NEW DIRECTIONS FOR CHILD

William Damon, *Stanford University*
EDITOR-IN-CHIEF

Development and Cultural Change: Reciprocal Processes

Elliot Turiel
University of California, Berkeley

EDITOR

Number 83, Spring 1999

JOSSEY-BASS PUBLISHERS
San Francisco

DEVELOPMENT AND CULTURAL CHANGE: RECIPROCAL PROCESSES
Elliot Turiel (ed.)
New Directions for Child and Adolescent Development, no. 83
William Damon, Editor-in-Chief

© 1999 by Jossey-Bass Inc., Publishers. All rights reserved.

No part of this issue may be reproduced in any form—except for a brief quotation (not to exceed 500 words) in a review or professional work—without permission in writing from the publishers.

Microfilm copies of issues and articles are available in 16mm and 35mm, as well as microfiche in 105mm, through University Microfilms Inc., 300 North Zeeb Road, Ann Arbor, Michigan 48106–1346.

ISSN 1520-3247   ISBN 0-7879-9845-1

NEW DIRECTIONS FOR CHILD AND ADOLESCENT DEVELOPMENT is part of The Jossey-Bass Education Series and is published quarterly by Jossey-Bass Inc., Publishers, 350 Sansome Street, San Francisco, California 94104–1342. Periodicals postage paid at San Francisco, California, and at additional mailing offices. Postmaster: Send address changes to New Directions for Child and Adolescent Development, Jossey-Bass Inc., Publishers, 350 Sansome Street, San Francisco, California 94104–1342.

New Directions for Child and Adolescent Development is indexed in Biosciences Information Service, Current Index to Journals in Education (ERIC), Psychological Abstracts, and Sociological Abstracts.

SUBSCRIPTIONS cost $67.00 for individuals and $115.00 for institutions, agencies, and libraries.

EDITORIAL CORRESPONDENCE should be sent to the Editor-in-Chief, William Damon, Stanford Center on Adolescence, Cypress Building C, Stanford University, Stanford, California 94305–4145.

Cover photograph by Wernher Krutein/PHOTOVAULT © 1990.

Jossey-Bass Web address: www.josseybass.com

Printed in the United States of America on acid-free recycled paper containing 100 percent recovered waste paper, of which at least 20 percent is postconsumer waste.

CONTENTS

EDITOR'S NOTES   1
Elliot Turiel

1. The Cognitive Context of Historical Change: Assimilation,   5
Accommodation, and the Segmentation of Competence
Wolfgang Edelstein
Change in the moral and cognitive realms is a long-term historical process that includes progression and regression.

2. Cognition, Development, and Cultural Practices   19
Geoffrey B. Saxe
Understanding the emergence of arithmetical thinking requires an analysis of dynamic relations between culture, cognition, and individual development.

3. Cultural Change and Human Development   37
Patricia M. Greenfield
Cultures change over time and result in changes in the process of learning and transmission.

4. Divergent Cultural Models of Child Rearing and Pedagogy   61
in Japanese Preschools
Susan D. Holloway
Diversity in educational philosophies and practices characterizes preschools in Japan, reflecting heterogeneity in the broader culture.

5. Conflict, Social Development, and Cultural Change   77
Elliot Turiel
Morality and personal autonomy in individual and collective understandings are sources of conflict and changes in cultural practices.

INDEX   93

Editor's Notes

The general theme of the chapters in this volume is the relation between culture and development. However, for many years there has been tension within the field of developmental psychology over how to explain development and how to explain people's participation in their cultures. Many have been concerned with the processes of individual thinking and development. That is, explanation of the development of the individual from infancy to childhood and on to adolescence and adulthood has been regarded as one of the central tasks of the field of psychology. Many psychologists have also been concerned with collectivities, or groupings of people over generations in cultures or societies. That is, explanation of how people are part of shared systems of values, beliefs, judgments, and practices also has been regarded as one of the central tasks of psychology. One of the salient tensions is between the emphasis on change in the individual's development and on stability and continuity in cultures.

A fair amount of this tension has focused on Piagetian theory. Piaget, many believe, largely neglected social and cultural influences on development and instead regarded the individual as developing in an autonomous, self-directed, and self-reliant way. It has become fashionable to highlight one of Piaget's examples (1971) to show that he was unconcerned with social activities and cultural influences (at least after his early work on moral judgments that emphasized the influences of peer interactions and cooperation). The example is a story told by one of Piaget's friends, who was a mathematician. The friend recounted that as a child he was counting pebbles one day and lined them up in a row. Counting from left to right he obtained the sum of ten. He then counted from right to left, and "was astonished that he got ten again." He then placed them in a circle, again counting to ten—first in one direction then the other.

As a child, Piaget's friend discovered that the sum is independent of the order (known in mathematics as commutativity). Piaget used the example to illustrate that knowledge can be derived from the coordination of actions. It was the child's actions on the objects (putting the pebbles in a line and a circle and counting in different directions) that allowed him to "abstract" from them (Piaget referred to this as simple abstraction in contrast to reflective abstraction). More generally, the purposes of this example were to illustrate how people can come to understandings and how thought and knowledge entail constructions, and to serve as a contrast to explanations of acquisition as being solely based on exogenous or biologically determined endogenous sources. Piaget's explanations of the development of thought were rooted in interactionism: in the experiences of the individual. The example of the child counting pebbles by himself was not meant to deny the significance of a coordination of actions that includes social interactions. It does suggest, however, that children engage in a variety of activities that influence development, including ones that may be reflective, individual, and social. It is true that Piaget did not explicate on collectivities that might constitute "culture" except in a set of essays on sociology written from 1928 to 1960 (Piaget, 1995).

We can see in the mainstays of cultural anthropology of the first half of the twentieth century a view of the exogenous sources of acquisition that contrasts with constructivism. Cultural anthropologists (for example, Benedict, 1934; Mead, 1928) then emphasized diversity and integration. They argued passionately for a recognition of diversity in the customs of the world, which they asserted could be "endlessly documented" (Benedict, 1934, p. 45) and which were associated with different cultures. The integration was identified in the patterns that cultures form: "The diversity of custom in the world, however, is not a matter which we can only helplessly chronicle . . . [cultural behavior] tends to also be integrated" (p. 46). Within cultures, individuals were presumed to be consistent in their thoughts and actions—a consistency based on the acquisition of the integrated patterns of one's culture: "The life-history of the individual is first and foremost an accommodation to the patterns and standards traditionally handed down in his community" (pp. 2–3).

It is informative to place those analyses into their historical context. Of particular importance is that cultural anthropologists were discontented with the ways cultural differences were often characterized. At the time, it was assumed by many that cultures could be ordered on a scale from less to more advanced. In many cases, those orderings were said to be based on evolution, and differences were attributed to genetics. Perhaps not coincidentally, the cultures of those proposing the orderings were placed at the most advanced or evolved levels. The cultural anthropologists were concerned that characterizing cultures in these ways reflected a bias in favor of one's own culture and that it failed to recognize the validity of diverse customs. They also pointed out that no criteria were provided for classifying a culture as more advanced than another. Cultural anthropologists proposed an alternative view: that cultures differ because of variations in patterns that are not comparable. A consequence of that view was that cultures were characterized as integrated and coherent, with accommodation on the part of individual participants. In turn, cultures were often presumed to be harmonious and stable. The emphasis on integration, coherence, and consistency, however, leaves out a great deal. It leaves out the conflicts and disagreements that occur within cultures. It also leaves out variations among people and contexts. Recently, there has been a reevaluation of the ideas of coherence and consistency on the part of several anthropologists, who maintain that analyses of any particular culture require attention to conflicts, diversity, and transformations over time (Abu-Lughod, 1991; Appadurai, 1988; Hatch, 1983; Spiro, 1993; Strauss, 1992; Wikan, 1991).

The chapters in this volume contribute to the reevaluation of the concept of culture. The writers are developmental and cultural psychologists who have been concerned with exploring the mutual influence of development and culture. In Chapter One, Wolfgang Edelstein takes a broad view of these issues by examining long-term historical changes in mathematics, legal systems, morality, and education. Although he argues for the idea of progress, he does not simply presume that changes over time constitute progress. Instead, he shows that change can be regressive or progressive. This makes for a more comprehensive understanding of change, one that draws important distinctions among types of change.

Change is also a focus of the chapters by Geoffrey B. Saxe (Chapter Two) and Patricia M. Greenfield (Chapter Three). Both of them relate individual cognition to cultural practices and consider the influences of changes in economic systems. The research discussed by Saxe bears mainly on concepts of number. He analyzes change in the number system and mathematical understandings of the Oksapmin in New Guinea brought about by new trade practices. Saxe links the research findings to a theory of form and function in three realms: microgenesis, ontogenesis, and sociogenesis. There are commonalities between Saxe's formulations and Greenfield's longitudinal studies of intergenerational change in the agrarian community of Zinacantan. Greenfield's research pertains to cognitive skills in the technology of weaving. Like Edelstein and Saxe, she proposes that cultures change over time. However, she further proposes that the processes of cultural learnings and transmission also change over time.

The chapter by Susan D. Holloway (Chapter Four) concerns variability and diversity within a culture. Her topic of study is Japanese preschools. In careful and detailed analyses of the philosophies of preschool directors and of the methods used, Holloway shows that Japanese preschools are not all of one kind. These characterizations are in sharp contrast with the portrayals that have emerged of the "typical" preschool and a homogeneous Japanese orientation.

My chapter (Chapter Five) also addresses the issue of intracultural variation. I consider variations stemming from the perspectives of people in different positions in the social hierarchy, and the relationship of hierarchy to moral and personal judgments. I propose that individuals' differing positions of power and influence result in multiple perspectives on cultural practices. Such varying perspectives often result in disagreements and conflicts, which can be sources of cultural changes.

The chapters in this volume confront the tensions, referred to previously, between psychologists' concerns with exploring development and with exploring participation in collectivities. Participation in cultures does entail acceptance of shared systems of values, judgments, and practices, but it also entails conflicts, contested meanings, and change. Change occurs among individuals and in cultures. The chapters in this volume examine individual development, cultural change, and reciprocal interactions of individuals and cultural arrangements.

Elliot Turiel
Editor

References

Abu-Lughod, L. "Writing Against Culture." In R. E. Fox (ed.), *Recapturing Anthropology: Working in the Present.* Santa Fe, N.M.: School of American Research Press, 1991.

Appadurai, A. "Putting Hierarchy in Its Place." *Cultural Anthropology,* 1988, *3,* 36–49.

Benedict, R. *Patterns of Culture.* Boston: Houghton Mifflin, 1934.

Hatch, E. *Culture and Morality: The Relativity of Values in Anthropology.* New York: Columbia University Press, 1983.

Mead, M. *Coming of Age in Samoa.* New York: Dell, 1928.

Piaget, J. *Genetic Epistemology.* New York: Norton, 1971.

Piaget, J. *Sociological Studies.* New York: Routledge, 1995.

Spiro, M. "Is the Western Conception of the Self 'Peculiar' Within the Context of the World Cultures?" *Ethos,* 1993, *21,* 107–153.

Strauss, C. "Models and Motives." In R. G. D'Andrade and C. Strauss (eds.), *Human Motives and Cultural Models.* New York: Cambridge University Press, 1992.

Wikan, U. "Towards an Experience-Near Anthropology." *American Anthropologist,* 1991, *6,* 285–305.

ELLIOT TURIEL *is Chancellor's Professor in the Graduate School of Education at the University of California, Berkeley.*

This chapter attempts to reconstruct the cognitive correlates of historical progress, using as examples the emergence of invariant numbers in Mesopotamia, the growth of logic and perspectivism in the early Middle Ages, and the rise of public education in the nineteenth century.

The Cognitive Context of Historical Change: Assimilation, Accommodation, and the Segmentation of Competence

Wolfgang Edelstein

For a long time we have relied, perhaps too uncritically, on the validity of what we might call cognitive progressivism. The message of cognitive progressivism runs as follows: the increasing cognitive complexity of the social order, and the heritage of European legal, social, and scientific enlightenment are bound to lead, through positive feedback, to further enhancement of cognitive competencies, both individual and collective. The challenge raised by social complexity is countered by increasing competence, by the enhanced quality of individual minds, and by greater universality and reversibility of collective judgments. In the wake of the Enlightenment, public education was optimistically assigned a major role in the enhancement of competencies. In the guise of welfare economics and human capital theory, the message of cognitive progressivism lasted into the seventies of this century and even became public policy during the heyday of socioeducational reform-mindedness in the member countries of the Organization for Economic Cooperation and Development (OECD) in the years of recovery after World War Two (Organization for Economic Cooperation and Development, 1960).

But considering recent historical experience, this view of cognitive progressivism seems too benign. Increased complexity is not automatically conducive to enhanced cognitive operations, let alone enhanced moral operations. A century ago, Durkheim ([1893] 1964) described the potentially negative corollaries and consequences of the sociocognitive complexity following the transition from what he called the "mechanical" solidarity (of a tribal and authoritarian social order) to the "organic" solidarity of a modern social order characterized by division of labor and complex cognitive and organizational social and institutional arrangements (Edelstein, 1983). The social, moral, and personal consequences of insufficient organizational and individual coping with the anomie of order lost in complexity may be dire: Durkheim ([1883] 1952) analyzes anomic suicide as a consequence of complexity-induced crisis. He calls for concerted action to prevent anomie and to lead the collective mind toward building higher-order solidarity in response to complexity. Durkheim ([1925] 1973) granted moral and political education in the public schools a prime role in this process.

Durkheim's observations have proved quite accurate. The century has seen spells of sociopolitical, institutional, and cognitive regression on a grand scale. Progressivists today suffer from acute hangover. Complexity, it now is apparent, works both ways: increasing pressure for assimilative response is but one; destructive regression, the violent simplification of complex structures, is another. In the face of regression, it is difficult to maintain confidence in an everlasting unfolding of individual cognitive competence as an assimilative response to the ever-growing cognitive complexity of social systems. The new fundamentalism testifies to the failure of cognitive progressivism as a sufficient theory of sociocultural evolution. So do the back-to-basics ideology in education and the new emphasis in political thought on ideas particular to social contexts. Universalist orientations are in doubt. A paradigm shift to relativism based on context is challenging the idea of progress. Communitarian thinkers, depending on their camp, have taken to the critique of universals as ideological, culturally erroneous, unnatural, or repressive. Thus, the Kantian heritage of cognitivistic universalism has yielded ground to postmodern relativism, a position shared by Derrida (Derrida and Caputo, 1996) and Shweder (1990; see Chandler, 1997).

It is necessary to face the challenge of contextualism and reconsider the possibility of progress in thought. It is one thing to critique the claims of progressivism and limit it to a position that is compatible with a more realistic and, at the same time, dialectical view of sociocognitive progress. It is quite another thing to abandon the notion of cognitive progress altogether. Although there are strong reasons, inside as well as outside psychology, to ponder the dialectics of enlightenment—the expression Horkheimer and Adorno (1972) chose for the inner contradictions and eventually the self-destruction of progress—there are equally strong reasons to refocus current analyses based on the idea that there cannot be progress in cognition. I plan to do so in this chapter by examining sociocognitive advances. In spite of the vicissitudes of progress there is the undeniable fact of cognitive evolution of the human species. On more local levels, we have a series of accounts that reconstruct the history of increasing cognitive complexity, stories of qualitative difference between prior (that is, more egocentric) and posterior (that is, more decentered) states and the transitions between them. In some instances the account may include mediating mechanisms or catalytic conditions that reinforce the growth of complexity and enhance the transition process. This is the story we recognize as universal in ontogenetic development as described by Piaget. Varieties of such dynamic processes have been described in structural terms at different levels of categorical explicitness, for example, in the context of the history of science (see Damerow, 1981, 1996); in the history of law and legal systems (Habermas, 1996); in the mechanisms of language change (de Saussure, 1993; Troubetckoy, 1967), and, as mentioned before, in the sociomoral constitution of modern societies (Durkheim, [1894] 1964).

Accounts of social and historical change are particularly interesting, as they portray the cooperation of human actors at different levels of complexity. This process of historical change implies the institutionalization of a cognitive tradition. The reflexive abstraction afforded by the sustained effort first to appropriate and then to transcend this tradition constitutes a collective learning process (Miller, 1986) that gradually (or, in some instances, suddenly) produces change. This process warrants particular attention when it is intentional—a planned attempt to put the cognitive process at the service of social, moral, or cultural goals. Following Durkheim ([1925] 1973), systems of education can be viewed, in part at least, as planned attempts to achieve a greater degree of collective competence and decentering. By calling on individuals to assimilate and appropriate a given symbolic order—a set of cognitive symbols or operators—the challenge to decenter is institutionalized as a cultural opportunity.

Although I wish to recapture a sense of the significance of sociocognitive progress, it would be Pollyannaish to ignore the contradictions and ambiguities of that progress. It is clearly mistaken to expect that the decentering follows automatically from the competence: for competence can be *segmented*—that is, foreclosed, defended against, barred from generalization, and functionally confined to a mere technical skill (Edelstein and Noam, 1982). Basically, the increased competence can be locked into a subsystem of cognitive functioning and thus deprived of its disequilibrating and reequilibrating potential, the power to generalize across the cognitive system. The segmentation of competence can explain the contradictions in thought that is not decentered. Everyday experiences with segmentation, overassimilation, or denial in individuals come to mind easily—the brilliant lawyer devoid of moral sense, the naive or narrow-minded scientist whose reasoning outside the realm of his competence defies his capacity, the skilled craftsman who is formal operational in the exercise of his skill—whereas the exercise of judgment may be restricted to structurally primitive stereotypes (see Piaget, 1972). The collective version of the segmentation processes, when competent individuals forfeit the exercise of competence but accept dominant paradigms of thought, is also well known: Kuhn's account of scientific revolutions (1965) demonstrates the inertial power and persistence of past paradigms. New findings that present anomalies are either excluded from the canonical paradigm or falsely subsumed, maintaining the protective belt of the prevailing structure. Milgram (1975) and Staub (1989) have reported impressive stories of the failure to make discerning judgments under pressure from persons in authority. The morally objectionable implications of action are segmented that is, prevented from transcending the narrow confines of a merely functional justification of the system of political or scientific constraints that authorized the action. Given the appropriate conditions, many or most individuals do not question the prevailing cognitive order or rule that regulates conduct in a subsystem of action even if it violates higher-order rules that would raise moral doubts about the justification of the action. Under the sway of authority, the rule guiding the action is segmented, while, confined to a circumscribed segment of behavior, the doubt that would undermine it is barred from generalization.

Typically, the construction of progress is long-term and evolutionary, equilibrating assimilation and accommodation over extended periods of time. In contrast, the breakdown of this process is sudden, sweeping, and revolutionary, although precursors may have been visible. Garcia (1992) has described in structural terms the natural process of sudden transition between aggregate states in nature. Horkheimer and Adorno's *Dialectic of Enlightenment* (1972) reflects the collective regression of advanced European societies into superstition, violence, and destruction as a response to social and economic contradictions. But these descriptions of social, economic, and cultural systems are far from adequate. We shall return to this question at the end of this chapter. (We do not discuss another view of the process of cognitive progress, which reads the very notion of progress as the history of loss and increasingly perfected domination; see Foucault, 1979, 1994.)

In the following sections, I offer three examples of historical transitions to more advanced collective competencies. The criteria used for identifying competencies are cognitive structures defined in cognitive developmental theory. The processes observed are reconstructed as progressions in a transition to a qualitatively different, more decentered state or stage. Space considerations demand that we make do with shortcut descriptions. Obviously, these can only provide quick glances, bird's-eye views, which by necessity must ignore the tortuous meandering of the course of historical processes. At the end of the chapter, I briefly consider the critical but ambiguous role of the school in cognitive progress.

The Emergence of Invariant Numbers in Mesopotamia

Peter Damerow (1981, 1996) has reconstructed the emergence in early Mesopotamia of a system of invariant numbers, and corresponding computation rules originating from variable units of representation of quantities, that were used for counting different categories of objects. Thus, for each relevant category of objects, quantification terms and counting procedures varied, in much the same way that in classificatory languages different pluralization systems obtain for given semantic objects (Benveniste, 1993).

In order to understand the meaning of the process toward invariance, we need to sensitize ourselves to the function of counting in the service of the accounting systems of the early Babylonian temple economy. Damerow suggests that the developmental pressure for the emergence of a unified system of invariant numbers that characterize quantities independent of the class of object counted or measured stems from the need to oversee and rationalize these bookkeeping operations. In the course of but a few hundred years in the third millennium B.C., the achievement of an invariant number system made possible an emergent system of computational operations that, viewed functionally, was gradually consolidated in the service of a complex system of bookkeeping and administration that regulated the economy, taxation, and commercial exchange, but simultaneously laid the structural foundation for the highly developed science of Babylonian mathematics. Damerow identified as an intermediary link the Babylonian scribes or accountants, who, responding to the challenge of their function strictly within a pragmatic context, over time developed exacting notational and computational rules. Babylonian mathematics arose from these rules and with time became dissociated from the administrative activities of the scribes and set out on a developmental course of its own (Damerow, 1981, 1996).

Damerow attributes great importance to the explanatory power of the sociocultural objects on which the agents of this process operate—the tools of the scribes, the system of notations, the social rules—that determine the scribes' roles and responsibilities. These sociocultural objects are intermediaries between the immediate object of cognition (the material objects submitted to the counting operations) and the developing cognitive system (the numbers and number operations). It is these intermediary object systems and the skills, actions, and behaviors involved in learning them and using them that make the cognitive representation (of numbers and operation on numbers) independent of the individuals concerned with them in any given case and that put distance between the operation and the mind. Thus they enable the mind to reflect on the operations and, ultimately, to develop them beyond individual representations of counting actions into a consistent and consolidated system of numbers and mathematical operations that can be acquired through planned learning independent of the functional context of the bureaucratic system.

The Growth of Logic and Perspectivism in the Middle Ages

Although the emergence of number invariance represents the paradigmatic case of contextualized yet general cognitive progression, historical processes of cognitive progression rarely have the transparent and circumscribed quality of the emergence of invariant number within the confines of a relatively simple social system (in our case, the temple economy of ancient Mesopotamia) (Nissen, 1988). The development of the symbolic regime of medieval culture presents a more complex case. In his enlightening book *A World Made by Men,* the historian Charles Radding (1985) traces intellectual development through the Middle Ages. Radding chooses a variety of dimensions for his demonstration of cognitive and sociocognitive development in and between the historical formations he analyzes. He traces the slow but pervasive change in systems of conflict resolution from the use of bodily actions, such as feuds or ordeals, as proofs of innocence to the use of cognitive actions, such as legal inquiry or jury deliberation.

Radding takes his basic inspiration for the reconstruction of mentality change from Piaget's study of the moral judgment of the child. This is a study, it will be remembered, of a game of marbles played by seven- to twelve-year-old boys in Geneva (Piaget, [1932] 1965). Piaget describes the progression from moral and cognitive realism, with rules considered absolute and external, to a reflexive and autonomous conception, where rules are tools of strategic cooperation, open, within limits, to negotiation.

For Radding, history's subjects are neither inert objects of institutions or rituals, nor functionally adaptive expressions of social or economical needs or laws; nor are they mere building bricks of collective mentalities, deprived of individual shape and intention. They are, like the players of the marble game, cognitively constructive *subjects.* Although we must learn from the cultural relativists that other times and other cultures differ from ours (and although we must indeed learn to decode that difference), we must also learn that history is peopled by reasoning individuals, who accommodate cognitive traditions and assimilate the schemata of their culture in their own individual but collectively validated ways.

In reconstructing the role of cognition in the shaping of European culture from the downfall of the Roman Empire into the twelfth century, Radding first describes how the rise of magical thinking had displaced or suppressed the classical traditions of reasoning. "Magic, both Christian and pagan, reigned supreme in attitudes towards the natural world, while in social thought conceptions of peer relations [in other words, the body politic] began to disappear, replaced by an ideal of hierarchy and authority. It is only 600 to 800 years later that substantive evidence is found for a break with this early medieval mentality" (1985, p. 55). Unfortunately, Radding does not deal with the processes of this intermediate regression. Yet it provides an important exemplar of the cognitive regression that represents the dark side of cognitive progressivism. Bent on explaining the process of cognitive advance he has traced in the texts, Radding identifies two local settings of great importance for the emergence of change: the cathedral school of Chartres and the law court of Pavia. Radding (pp. 255–256) explains:

> The conditions of debate in these traditional milieus had changed in two subtle ways. The first was the result of the long-term rise in educational standards, which by increasing the number of educated people accentuated the impact of any dispute (gradualism). The second was the collapse of political order in many parts of Europe that made appeal to outside authority impossible (closed sys-

tem). Thrown back on their own resources, people had to learn again the skills of persuading each other, and they responded by finding more skillful ways of reading texts, by insisting upon logical consistency as a foundation of argument and by taking more account of the views of those with whom they disagreed.

Thus, gradual and cumulative increase in individual competence in interaction with a set of systemic conditions produced the progressive change that represents a new stage of collective intellectual and institutional development.

In the closing part of his book, Radding traces the effects of the new cognition on twelfth-century society. "Intellectual discourse, which had long consisted chiefly of citations from authorities, was reconstructed on the basis of *logic,* and this was just one of the ways in which education changed towards being a creative [that is, constructive] instead of a curatorial process. No less important were the changes worked in social institutions. Law and politics became affairs of the community [in other words, a cooperative process] and not just the king alone, while in the monasteries a similar process encouraged the religiously inclined to seek expression of their interior feelings in the company of equals" (p. 256). A dynamic of mutual assimilation takes place here, involving both individuals and the institutions they serve. By using their cognitive potential, individuals and institutions foster each other's development.

In this analysis, various pieces of a cognitively based dynamic of change are in evidence: peer discussion, logical contradiction, the need to establish logical consistency, and the authority of logic; the dissolution of the auctorial tradition in favor of a mentality that appeals to the role of reasoning in order to establish truth, and the challenge this poses to a conciliatory understanding of the texts; the adoption initially of a second-person and ultimately of a third-person perspective in order to conduct a persuasive argument; and finally, the complex and subtle infusion into education of all facets of this process, leading to a gradual transformation that turned education into an instrument for cultivation of cognitive discriminations.

In central domains of social life, such as vassalage (the institution representing the basic political relationship of government) and marriage (the institution organizing "private" life), a qualitative transformation toward perspectivism, reciprocity, intentionality, and mutuality, and a discursive establishment of subjective entitlement is in evidence (at least in precursor exemplars that set the trend). This is not to say that the world changes completely when mentalities show signs of change. But it is clear, for example, from the poetry of courtly love, from the rituals of chivalry, from the distinctions of theology, and from the canons of education that, partly by the tenth, more by the twelfth, and certainly by the thirteenth century, the cognitive, logical, and moral constitution of the social order and the corresponding reciprocal expectations of individuals had undergone far-reaching transformations from, say, the earlier Middle Ages.

But Radding does not devote much thought to the other side of the process: that earlier established cognitive structures and mentalities had broken down almost completely before the "process of civilization" (Elias, 1978) started to renew the crude structures of thought and interaction that characterized the early Middle Ages. Radding does not ask how the highly developed cognitive structures characteristic of the Roman Empire disintegrated and disappeared. Nor does he devote much space to the demonstration of *décalage,* the existence of different levels of development in a given period. There is a considerable literature that deals with the survival of ideas from Roman antiquity after the transition into the early Middle Ages (Curtius, 1993); and there is bound to be survival of prior, less developed cognitive stances among groups and individuals and to be discontinuities among subpopulations both in the opportunities and in the capacity to access the new cognitive order. Yet these differences between individuals and groups are important if we are to gauge the degree of consolidation a cognitive structure has reached its success as a pervasive mentality. And it is tempting to speculate that increasing pressure for widespread availability of higher-level cognitive skills would ultimately lead to the establishment of education as a device that institutionalized individual access to formal cognitive skills and simultaneously diminished the extent of *arbitrary* individual differences in cognitive competence. But it took centuries to develop acts of royal legislation to promote universal education.

The Division of Labor and the Ascendancy of Universal Education

Notwithstanding the cognitive transformations that led away from the realism and relative lack of perspective taking characteristic of early medieval mentality, the cognitive and sociomoral requirements for mastering the work and relationship system of postmedieval (but still traditional) premodern society remained much less complex than are the cognitive demands on the individual in modern societies. It is, of course, not possible to detail here the cognitive bases of traditional and modern societies in a comparative perspective. But in order to understand the transition to modern society, with its immensely complex cognitive requirements, one must grasp the cognitive structure of premodern societies. Elsewhere I have described what I take to be the cognitive implications of traditional patterns of life using the example of sheep-raising farms in premodern Iceland (Edelstein, 1983). The society is based, as is the case in all traditional subsistence econômies, on a stable and recurrent or cyclical pattern of occurrences and experiences, where the nature of the experience of one generation is similar to both that of the preceding generation and the following: the same seasons, the same crops, the same actions and activities, the same tools and instruments, the same type of exchanges, and the same rituals, which punctuate the cycle of seasons as well as the cycle of human life. The recurrent pattern makes the structure of lived experience transparent and comprehensible. The functional relevance of required actions is never in doubt; every piece in the pattern has its circumscribed meaning, so that no ulterior motive is needed.

Durkheim, in his classic of sociology, *The Division of Labor in Society* ([1893] 1964), contrasted this "segmented" pattern of traditional social organization with the modern form of divided labor. The type of social relationships in segmented (that is, "primitive," or traditional) societies he calls *mechanical solidarity*, relationships that depend on similarity and affinity between functions (the form of a collection). In posttraditional societies the division of labor is based on the coordination of different functions, an abstract mode of cooperation producing what Durkheim calls *organic solidarity*. Durkheim shows that the two types of social organization correspond with different patterns of normative regulations. Whereas mechanical solidarity calls on ritualistic and conventional regulations, the division of labor in a modern society pulls for the systems of modern law and postconventional morality. Under organic solidarity, complex moral regulations, symbolic exchanges, and a third-person perspective on the social adequacy of actions are needed to maintain an abstract order that is grounded on a regime of functional differences and complements. But in Durkheim's functionalism, the emergent social structures do not automatically generate the corresponding moral motives. A conscious and reflective mind is needed to construct the moral solidarity required to maintain collective order among individuals who, although linked to each other in a relationship of complex production and exchange, represent individuality and difference, remain socially alien to each other, and stress the subjectivity of experience. These processes are brought about through *moral education*, a device for the production of loyalty to the structure of the whole, which, by way of respect for the individual, reaches beyond the individuals to the ensemble they constitute. It is the abstract moral community that warrants the dignity of each and any of its members, who, by contributing their individuality to that community, represent it in its entirety and completeness (Durkheim, [1925] 1973).

Interestingly, Durkheim, in his treatise on education, spelled out the moral, not cognitive, implications of modern social organization. Even when viewing education primarily as a means for moral change, we cannot ignore the cognitive functions of curriculum and instruction, the systematic and planned transmission of knowledge. In traditional society, knowledge was stable, unchanging, and valid across generations. The transmission process accordingly called for authoritative reproduction. In modern societies, knowledge is incremental, transformational, and innovative. Its structure is increasingly formal, relational, and generative. The undoubted authority of tradition vouching for truth yields to methodological doubt and systematic critique as truth-producing procedures. Particular adaptations to particular cultures that are based on concrete and immediate experience acquired through participation are replaced by general laws and regularities. To put it a different way: experiential adaptation to functional roles and situated learning in a local culture is replaced by formal instruction as the defining cognitive experience (Edelstein, 1983).

Whereas cognitive experience in traditional societies operates on the concrete and therefore generates largely adaptive solutions, once the acquisition process of cognitive experience has been locked into institutions designed for abstract, nonsituated learning as a practice of its own, cognitive experience is transformed. It is no longer concrete, direct, and participatory but is instead vicarious and intentionally designed as a cognitive experience. It therefore represents an experience of abstraction from immediate experience. No longer is it a response to a functional challenge in the real world; it is now a design to serve the acquisition process itself. The goal of learning is learning, an operation on operations.

Historically speaking, this process has been immensely effective. The introduction of compulsory schooling for everybody, beginning in Prussia in the late eighteenth century, made available to almost everybody, independent of economic status and social origin, a set of cognitive operations linked to the manipulation of letters and numbers. In due time it would provide elements of scientific reasoning, and contributions toward an information-oriented mentality were to follow. A mentality that prizes the acquisition of information for its own sake places a premium on assimilation. The mind is pressed (and rewarded) to become operational on the basis of an institutionalized process of knowledge acquisition that depends on a heuristic and an economy of its own, neither unequivocally authority-bound nor naturally exploratory.

The Dynamic of Segmentation

The school as a knowledge-generating device has contradictory effects. On the one hand, it has driven the process of cognitive empowerment to unprecedented lengths by offering cognitive competence to increasing numbers of individuals independent of the constraints of natural experience. In this respect it stands in the service of liberation from the bondage of illiteracy throughout the world. On the other hand, school as a specific organization for the acquisition of knowledge is based on the dissociation of experience and learning, whose very conjunction had defined development before the advent of universal education. Thus education represents a new kind of socioeconomic and cultural bondage: the dependency of an effective conduct of life on school success.

At this juncture it would be necessary to study the emergent dynamic of segmentation that constrains both individual learning and the school as an institution. Although cognitive motivation is always aroused in a functional exploration of an experiential challenge (Berlyne, 1960; Piaget, 1972; White, 1959), this may not be the case when experience is vicarious and compulsory. School learning, for this reason among others, is beset by the problem of motivation. The separation of learning from experience and the denaturalization of learning that comes with its institutionalization in schools have generated a deficit of cognitive motivation. This may be a relatively new problem in history, for which no reliable cure has been devised, in spite of incessant attempts at school reform (Edelstein, 1995). With some simplification, it can be maintained that school reforms since Dewey have been designed to attack this problem by substituting equivalents for direct experience to enhance motivated processes of constructive learning.

The results have been less than convincing, because for a variety of reasons, attempts at reforming the process of school learning have not been successful in renaturalizing learning as a functional and developmentally effective experiential activity. Nor have teachers been able to adjust their roles to the support of such processes. The compulsory school as designed for the masses has continued to rely for its success on the accommodation of the learners to school and instruction that used to function well enough for elites whose motivation was nurtured at home and for social and economic goals beyond the purposes of schooling. The present imperative of mass schooling calls for the accommodation of instruction to the students' processes of exploration. The variance in students' socialized ability to accommodate the school has produced a specific set of individual differences among learners, with success mostly reserved for those who are able to forego natural epistemic conditions for learning. Perhaps the most powerful invention to serve the cognitive advance in the species (Bruner, 1966) therefore has produced ambiguous results: by liberating cognitive development from the natural constraints of the acquisition process, by being designed entirely for the provision of knowledge, by separating learning from its natural (that is, experiential) source, by providing an institution, school has also locked the knowledge acquisition process into the shackles of institutionalized learning. Given the corresponding systemic conditions, this may well be an avenue toward cognitive regression rather than progression (Edelstein, 1983).

In summary, there is overwhelming evidence for cognitive progress throughout history. The history of science and the history of mechanics and its many applications give ample credence to this idea. So does knowledge about the social and organizational evolution of work, the organizational patterns of cooperation, and the changing structures of social and administrative systems. Increasing complexity, indeed, has continually given rise to higher levels of cognitive coordination. However, organizational complexity and the accompanying cognitive complexity needed to manage it have generated contradictions in the very systems they have brought forth: Durkheim, almost one hundred years ago, wrote a classical analysis of the need for a new form of moral responsibility—organic solidarity—to replace a traditional morality of kinship and authority rules. Organic solidarity is based on individual responsibility within functional variability of roles in a cognitively complex and dynamic order. The need for the new form of moral responsibility stemmed from increased socio-organizational and cognitive complexity accompanying the transition to a modern society characterized by the division of labor. Horkheimer and Adorno (1972), notwithstanding a different theoretical stance, follow the negative dynamics of this process beyond the stage described by Durkheim toward the self-destruction of rationality and a rational social order. Whether school—the central institution designed to serve the knowledge-acquisition and knowledge-processing imperatives of cognitively and organizationally complex modern societies—is able to contribute to the construction of the organic solidarity needed to cope with the contradictory potential of action in complex social systems or will fail to do so due to the inner contradictions of schooling (Edelstein, 1995) remains a moot question.

References

Benveniste, E. *Problèmes de linguistique générale* [Problems of general linguistics]. Paris: Gallimard, 1993.
Berlyne, D. E. *Conflict, Arousal, and Curiosity*. New York: McGraw-Hill, 1960.
Bruner, J. S. *Towards a Theory of Instruction*. Cambridge, Mass.: Belknap Press, 1966.
Chandler, M. "Stumping for Progress in a Post-Modern World." In E. Amsel and K. A. Renniger (eds.), *Change and Development: Issues of Theory, Method, and Application*. Mahwah, N.J.: Erlbaum, 1997.
Curtius, E. R. *Europäische Literatur und lateinisches Mittelalter* [European literature and the Latin Middle Ages]. Tübingen, Germany: Francke, 1993.
Damerow, P. "Die Entstehung des arithmetischen Denkens" [The origins of arithmetical reasoning]. In P. Damerow and W. Lefèvre (eds.), *Rechenstein, Experiment, Sprache* [Calculus, experiment, language]. Stuttgart, Germany: Klett-Cotta, 1981.
Damerow, P. *Abstraction and Representation: Essays on the Cultural Evolution of Thinking*. Boston: Kluwer, 1996.
Derrida, J., and Caputo, J. D. *Deconstruction in a Nutshell: A Conversation with Jacques Derrida*. New York: Fordham University Press, 1996.
Durkheim, E. *Suicide*. New York: Routledge, 1952. (Originally published 1883.)
Durkheim, E. *The Division of Labor in Society*. New York: Free Press, 1964. (Originally published 1893.)
Durkheim, E. *Moral Education: A Study in the Theory and Application of the Sociology of Education*. New York: Free Press, 1973. (Originally published 1925.)
Edelstein, W. "Cultural Constraints on Development and the Vicissitudes of Progress." In F. S. Kessel and A. W. Siegel (eds.), *The Child and Other Cultural Inventions*. New York: Praeger, 1983.
Edelstein, W. "Universal Functions in Particular Systems: A Developmental View of Educational Regulation in Closed Educational Systems." In P. M. Roeder, I. Richter, and H.-P. Füssel (eds.), *Pluralism and Education: Current World Trends in Policy, Law, and Administration*. Berkeley, Calif.: Institute of Governmental Studies Press, 1995.
Edelstein, W., and Noam, G. "Regulatory Structures of the Self and 'Postformal' Stages in Adulthood." *Human Development*, 1982, 25, 407–422.
Elias, N. *The Civilizing Process*. Oxford: Blackwell, 1978.
Foucault, M. *Discipline and Punish: The Birth of the Prison*. New York: Vintage Books, 1979.
Foucault, M. *The Birth of the Clinic: An Archaeology of Medical Perception*. New York: Vintage Books, 1994.
Garcia, R. "The Structure of Knowledge and the Knowledge of Structure." In H. Beilin and P. Pufall (eds.), *Piaget's Theory*. Mahwah, N.J.: Erlbaum, 1992.
Habermas, J. *Between Facts and Norms: Contributions to a Discourse Theory of Law and Democracy*. Cambridge, Mass.: MIT Press, 1996.
Horkheimer, M., and Adorno, T. W. *Dialectic of Enlightenment*. New York: Herder & Herder, 1972.
Kuhn, T. S. *The Structure of Scientific Revolutions*. Chicago: University of Chicago Press, 1965.
Milgram, S. *Obedience to Authority*. New York: HarperCollins, 1975.
Miller, M. *Kollektive Lernprozesse* [Collective learning processes]. Frankfurt, Germany: Suhrkamp, 1986.

Nissen, H. J. *The Early History of Ancient Near East, 9000–2000 B.C.* Chicago: University of Chicago Press, 1988.
Organization for Economic Cooperation and Development. *Targets for Education.* Paris: Organization for Economic Cooperation and Development, 1960.
Piaget, J. *The Moral Judgment of the Child.* New York: Free Press, 1965. (Originally published 1932.)
Piaget, J. *The Child and Reality: Problems of Genetic Psychology.* New York: Grossmann, 1972.
Radding, C. M. *A World Made by Men: Cognition and Society, 400–1200.* Chapel Hill: University of North Carolina Press, 1985.
Saussure, F. de. *Course in General Linguistics* (C. Bally, ed.). London: Duckworth, 1993.
Shweder, R. A. "Cultural Psychology: What Is It?" In J. W. Stigler, R. A. Shweder, and G. Herdt (eds.), *Cultural Psychology: Essays on Comparative Human Development.* New York: Cambridge University Press, 1990.
Staub, E. *The Roots of Evil: The Origins of Genocide and Other Group Violence.* New York: Cambridge University Press, 1989.
Troubetckoy, N. S. *Principes de phonologie* [Principles of phonology]. Paris: Klincksieck, 1967.
White, R. W. "Motivation Reconsidered: The Concept of Competence." *Psychological Review,* 1959, 56, 297–333.

WOLFGANG EDELSTEIN is director emeritus of the Max Planck Institute for Human Development and Education in Berlin, where until June 1997 he directed the Center of Development and Socialization.

This chapter presents a developmental framework for the study of culture and cognition in which cultural practice is a key organizing construct.

Cognition, Development, and Cultural Practices

Geoffrey B. Saxe

In this chapter, I sketch a research approach for gaining insight into relations between culture and cognition, with a focus keyed to the overarching theme of this volume—the interplay between cognitive development and cultural change.

Treatments of cultural change and cognitive development are often linked to different disciplines, analyses of cognitive development belonging to psychology and analyses of culture and cultural change linked to sociology and cultural anthropology. Like others who have broken with this disciplinary tradition, I argue that a systematic analysis of either cultural change or cognitive development requires that they be understood relative to one another in a single integrative treatment. (Other authors who make similar arguments include Cole, 1997; Luria, 1976; Scribner, 1985; Wertsch, 1991; and Patricia Greenfield in Chapter Three of this volume.) A core thesis is that a wide range of cognitive developments take form in and depend on cultural practices and that new developments in culture (cultural change) involve the cognitive constructions of individuals.

Some Preliminaries

The approach I outline is *cultural* in that it identifies collective practices as integral to understanding the interrelationships between cultural change and cognitive change. Practices are conceptualized broadly as recurrent, socially organized activities that permeate daily life (Scribner and Cole, 1981). Practices may be as diverse as playing games, working in particular professions, or participating in any of a diverse set of social institutions (school, religion, or politics). Regardless of the practice, the approach assumes that there is a reflexive relation between individual activities and collective practices. Individuals' cognitive activities are constitutive of practices, and at the same time practices give form and social meaning to individuals' activities.

The approach is also *developmental*. A core assumption is that novel cognitive developments emerge in individuals' efforts to structure and accomplish goals in practices. The focus is on three levels of analysis, each of which concerns the interplay between *cultural forms*, such as number systems, and *cognitive functions*, the purposes for which forms are used as individuals structure and accomplish practice-linked goals. The analyses concern processes of (1) microgenesis, or cognitive changes that occur as individuals transform cultural forms into cognitive means for representing and accomplishing goals in practices; (2) ontogenesis, or shifting relations between individuals' uses of particular forms and functions in practices as the grow older; and (3) sociogenesis, or changes that occur in cultural forms as individuals' representational and strategic accomplishments become valued by other members of a community and spread to serve variant functions in individuals' practice-related goals.

Readers familiar with formulations of cognitive development will find that the cultural-developmental approach sketched here is marked by a confluence of Piagetian and Vygotskian ideas. Key Piagetian constructs of epigenesis (that new structures of knowledge have their roots in prior structures) and construction (that individuals are active agents in epigenetic change) are central to the treatment of development (Piaget, 1970). At the same time, Piaget's focus on universals does not well afford a differentiated treatment of history and culture in analyses of cognitive development, a principal focus here. In this regard, the approach shows similarities with Vygotsky's focus on mediation as a key target in an analysis of the intrinsic relations between individual and social history in a treatment of development (Vygotsky, 1978, 1986).

The Changing Practice of Economic Exchange in the Oksapmin

In sketching the framework, I draw on one of my prior studies on arithmetic of a remote group in Papua New Guinea—the Oksapmin of the West Sepik Province (Saxe, 1982). I target the practice of economic exchange as it is conducted by adults. The example presents a remarkable instance in which the dynamics of cultural change and development stand out in particularly clear relief. My focus is on the emerging arithmetic used by the Oksapmin as it is linked to ongoing shifts in the practice of economic exchange.

The Oksapmin Setting and Traditional Practices Involving Number. The Oksapmin people live in a remote highlands area. The only means of access is by foot and by single-engine aircraft. For subsistence, Oksapmin people use slash-and-burn methods to cultivate taro and sweet potato, use bows and arrows to hunt for small game, and keep pigs. Western contact was first established with the Oksapmin by the Australian 1938–1940 Hagen-Sepik

COGNITION, DEVELOPMENT, AND CULTURAL PRACTICES   21

patrol, although it was not until the 1950s that the Oksapmin were contacted by additional patrols. A government patrol post and a mission station were established in the Oksapmin area in the early 1960s.

The standard Oksapmin number system differs markedly from the Western base-ten system, as do the systems of other Papua New Guinea groups (see Lancy, 1983). To count as Oksapmin do, one begins with the thumb on one hand and enumerates twenty-seven places around the upper periphery of the body, ending on the little finger of the opposite hand. If one needs to count further, one can continue back up to the wrist of the second hand and progress back upward on the body (see Figure 2.1).

Oksapmin Practices of Economic Exchange. Contact with the West has led to shifts in the everyday practices with which Oksapmin are engaged, including practices involving economic exchange and number. In traditional practices, Oksapmin used the body system to count valuables (for example, pigs), to denote the ordinal position of an element in a series of elements (for example, the ordinal position of a hamlet in a series of hamlets on a path), or in basic measurement operations (for example, as a means of measuring and representing the length of string bags, a common cultural artifact). Procedures for computation are not used in traditional life; however, there are some analogs of a computational process. For instance, in traditional economic exchanges, Oksapmin traded goods directly in one-for-one or one-for-many exchanges (bows for leaves of salt, axes for bows). In general, such analogs lack a representational solution procedure in which an answer can be determined in the absence of the objects.

Figure 2.1. The Oksapmin Body-Part Counting System

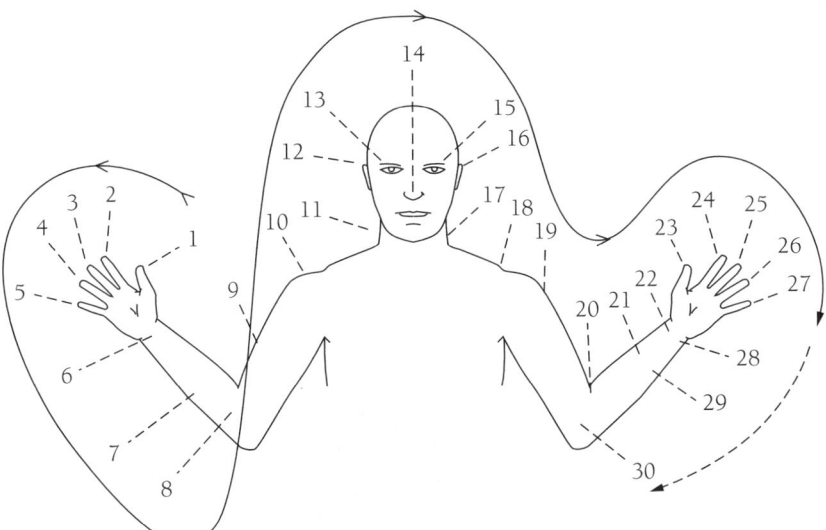

The brief history of Western currency in the Oksapmin community is noteworthy, as it has relevance to understanding the shifting practice of economic exchange and the way Oksapmin come to structure and accomplish numerical goals in economic transactions. Western currency entered the Oksapmin community through a number of routes. Australian shillings and pounds (20 shillings equaling 1 pound) were brought by early missionaries and patrol officers to the region, in about 1961. In 1966, the Australian dollar was instituted (100 cents equaling 1 dollar); and in 1975, before the country became independent, Papua New Guinea issued its own currency in the form of kina and toea (200 toea equaling one 2-kina note). Beginning in the 1960s, some Oksapmin men were flown out of the area to earn about 200 kina (the equivalent of about $300 in purchasing value) for two-year stints of labor on copra and tea plantations. These men often returned to the Oksapmin community; some built tiny trade stores and bought bags of rice and cans of fish to sell to people in their hamlets. The first trade store was started in 1972, and by 1980 there were more than one hundred stores in the subdistrict. These stores are the contexts in which currency is exchanged most frequently within the Oksapmin community. Missionaries and government officers continue to contribute to the local supply of currency through the purchase of vegetables or through the trading of currency for labor (such as the carrying of goods). Many Oksapmin people, particularly individuals beyond their twenties, translate kina and toea (the current national currency) into pounds and shillings (the first currency system). On this basis, people call one 10-toea coin, 1 shilling. (A 20-toea coin is called 2 shillings and one 2-kina note, 1 pound.)

Analyzing Development in Oksapmin Arithmetic: Relations Between Form and Function

I reasoned that economic transactions in such sites as trade stores led individuals to create numerical goals and that these goals differ from those that mark traditional economic practices. For instance, in the trade store, customer and owner pose arithmetical problems to one another. The customer presents items to be purchased for currency while the store owner evaluates the amount of those items and considers payment in currency for those items. To understand the way changes in the practices in which individuals engage are related to form-function shifts in individuals' efforts to achieve these goals, I observed and interviewed people with varying levels of participation in the money economy. In the interviews, I was concerned with learning about individuals' use of the body-system form in problems that emerged in such contexts and the way use varied with increasing participation in such currency-linked exchanges.

The fruits of the observations and interviews led to the identification of the three interrelated levels of developmental analysis noted earlier—microgenesis, ontogenesis, and sociogenesis. In each case, cognition is understood as a process undergoing transformation as cultural forms, such as the Oksapmin number system, become vehicles for serving new functions in currency-based economic practices.

Microgenesis. The meanings of cultural forms are not fixed. In everyday Oksapmin practices, for example, body parts are only sometimes used to signify numerical relations. At other times, pointing to body parts simply refers to parts of the body. Even when body parts are used as numerical signifiers, numerical meanings are not predetermined, but take form in activity. For example, the same body part may refer to different numbers, because sometimes individuals count from right to left and at other times from left to right. Further, body parts are sometimes used to refer to ordinal numbers and at other times to cardinal numbers. Thus, cultural forms like the body system are schematized to serve different functions as they are used in activities. This schematization involves a process of microgenesis in which the body-part form is transformed into a means for accomplishing goals in practices.

Werner and Kaplan (1962) proposed a model of microgenesis that can be extended to the analysis of numerical reference in Oksapmin. The model provides a means of understanding how referential meaning and semiotic flexibility are possible in cognitive activities (for example, how, at one moment, the individual can use the nose to mean the number fourteen and in the next moment use the nose to mean the body part that was the source of a sneeze). As used here, the model consists of three aspects. These involve a schematization of (1) a representational vehicle, such as a number or other system of reference; (2) a representational object, such as the quantity of objects in a set; and (3) a semantic mapping between vehicle and object. These activities are assumed to occur coextensively. Here, we consider the problem of numerical reference in Oksapmin.

Schematizing a Vehicle for Numerical Reference. If cultural forms have no inherent numerical meaning, how do they become symbolic vehicles that take on numerical meaning? Werner and Kaplan point out that forms (such as body parts) have "latent" features that can afford or support a wide range of cognitive functions. For instance, fingers are elongated, and the elbow is hard and pointed. Such latent features are brought to the foreground in activity as they are deployed to serve particular functions—the fingers and thumb may be used to serve prehensile functions, and the elbow may be used to jab. The same body parts also have latent features that can be brought to the fore to serve numerical functions in convenient ways: body parts can be parsed and ordered as a stable sequence and organized in a pattern (up one side of the body and down the other). These latent features also constrain numerical functions in particular ways. For example, one can only count to relatively small numbers using body parts. Such latent features mean that even though body parts have no intrinsic numerical function, they can be schematized in such a fashion that they serve numerical functions.

Schematizing an Object of Numerical Reference. Just as body parts are not inherently numerical, elements in the world that are the target of numerical representations have no inherent numerical meaning. However, like body parts, objects have latent features that can be used to support quantitative activity. To be treated numerically, objects must be schematized as discrete entities that are countable. For instance, objects (such as Oksapmin pigs) can be treated one by one and conceptualized as a countable set.

Schematizing Relations Between Vehicle and Object. Finally, to use body parts to represent objects numerically requires not only that a potential vehicle (body part) and a potential object of representation (pig, shell, coin) be schematized as conceptual entities with numerical properties but also that a relation between body parts and target entities be created coextensively, such that each body part denotes a potential sum of objects (the forearm may be used to refer to the totality of seven pigs) or a potential position in an enumeration (the forearm may be used to denote the seventh pig); indeed, without a schematization of a one-to-one correspondence between vehicle and object, the vehicle does not provide a means of representing the object numerically. Thus, inherent in the microgenetic act is a schematization of a correspondence between the latent qualities of the vehicle and object such that one can come to stand for the other.

An Example of the Microgenesis of an Arithmetical Strategy Linked to Economic Exchange with Currency. Consider a traditional adult who participates little in the money economy, as he attempts to solve the following problem: "You have six shillings [one shilling equals one coin]," as the informant gestures around the body to the appropriate body part and to the coins. "A friend gives you eight shillings" (gesturing from the thumb to the inner elbow). "How many do you have altogether?"

As depicted in Figure 2.2, to accomplish the problem, the individual enumerates body parts beginning with the thumb (1) and ending at the wrist (6) to represent six coins (the first term of the problem). For the second addend (eight), the individual continues with his count, not creating a means of keeping track of the addition of eight on to six, thus stopping at an inappropriate body part, the ear on the other side (16). The failure to keep track makes sense when we consider that in traditional practices, arithmetic with nonpresent objects was virtually nonexistent. Thus, when confronted with the novel arithmetical task, the individual treats the activity as if it were a count of present objects, in which keeping track does not emerge as a problem with which to be dealt.

Figure 2.3 contains a general depiction of the microgenetic process. The figure shows the threefold schematization involved in the count of six plus eight coins. The individual begins with the intent to produce a cardinal representation—a numerical function afforded by the body system. The individual brings to bear his knowledge of the body system, a cultural form to serve a numerical function—the representation of a cardinal value. The function is realized in an effort to accomplish the goal of representing numerically the first term of the problem. In this representational act, the individual structures an imaginary one-to-one correspondence between vehicle and object of reference such that the body parts become a vehicle for representing coins. In

COGNITION, DEVELOPMENT, AND CULTURAL PRACTICES   25

Figure 2.2. A Global Enumeration Procedure Used to Solve the Problem 6 + 8 = ?

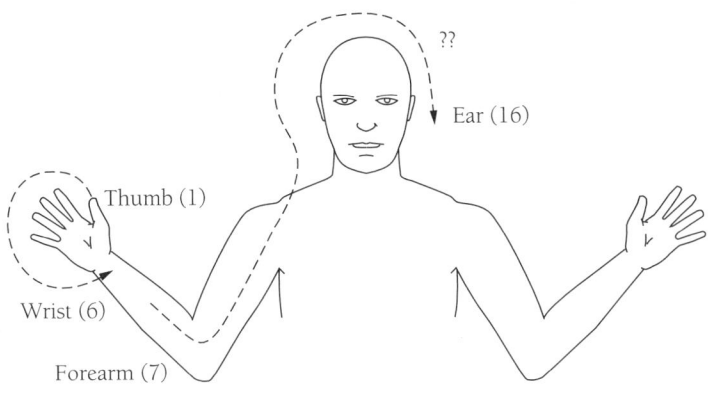

Figure 2.3. The Microgenesis of a Global Enumeration Procedure

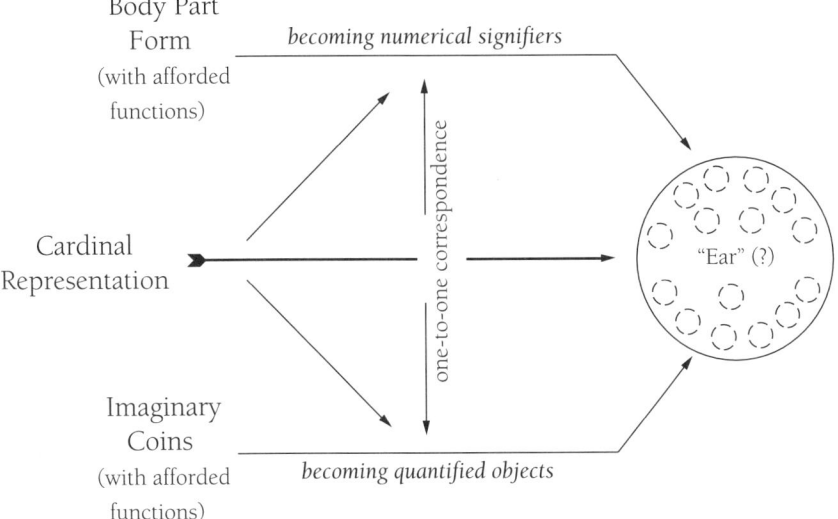

this process, the generic form of body parts becomes parsed into ordered numerical symbols, and the imaginary coins are coextensively parsed into a group of elements to be enumerated. In the end, the product of the activity is the wrist, the symbolic expression referring to six coins. To add the additional coins, the individual continues the flow of the microgenetic process of structuring a representational solution to the arithmetical problem by schematizing imaginary coins from the forearm (7), though the schematization is not adequate to produce an accurate solution.

In this sketch of microgenesis, individuals structure cultural forms like the body system into means for accomplishing representational and strategic goals. This dynamic process allows for the flexibility of forms to serve different functions in activity, in that the same forms may be structured into means for accomplishing different ends. Such flexibility may be fundamental for individuals' construction of novel cognitive developments over the course of ontogenetic change, an issue addressed next.

Ontogenesis. To gain insight into developmental shifts in the way individuals approached and accomplished arithmetical problems over time, I used a cross-sectional method. I interviewed eighty individuals who varied in their levels of participation with the money economy. These included men who had owned a trade store for at least two years, men who had returned from a period of work at a plantation but did not own a trade store, young adults who had not been to a plantation (and therefore had little experience with currency), and older adults who had not been to a plantation and who therefore had only peripheral experience with the money economy. I reasoned that an analysis of these individuals' strategies (microgenetic constructions) would provide insight into the way engagement in the practice of economic exchange supports new kinds of microgenetic constructions, reflecting more sophisticated correspondence operations.

The double-enumeration strategy depicted in Figure 2.4 appears to be an outgrowth of the global enumeration procedure used by the traditional adult described in the earlier example. With the double-enumeration strategy, individuals created a more differentiated schematization of a problem solution. To solve the same problem (six plus eight coins), an individual begins at the first term of the problem (wrist, 6). As the individual adds the second term (elbow, 8), he keeps a record by establishing physical correspondences with a subseries of body parts used to represent the second term (thumb, 1, to inner elbow, 8). Thus, the individual establishes correspondences between the thumb (1) and the forearm (7), the first finger (2) and the inner elbow (8), and so on until the individual reaches the correspondence between the inner elbow (8) and the nose (14). As a result, unlike the earlier global strategy, the individual typically achieves the accurate answer, nose (14).

Figure 2.5 contains a depiction of the microgenesis of the double-enumeration strategy. The figure highlights both the continuity and discontinuity with the prior global enumeration approach. One-to-one correspondences are used again (continuity); however, in the double-enumeration strategy, these correspondences are used to serve a new function (discontinuity). Indeed, the focus of activity becomes the creation of secondary correspondences that coordinate the addition of the two addends into a sum. One-to-one correspondences between body parts and coins remain implicit in the microgenetic process, providing the basis of numerical meaning for each addend.

A further development is the body-part substitution strategy (depicted in Figure 2.6). This schematization is similar to the double-enumeration

COGNITION, DEVELOPMENT, AND CULTURAL PRACTICES   27

Figure 2.4. The Double-Enumeration Procedure

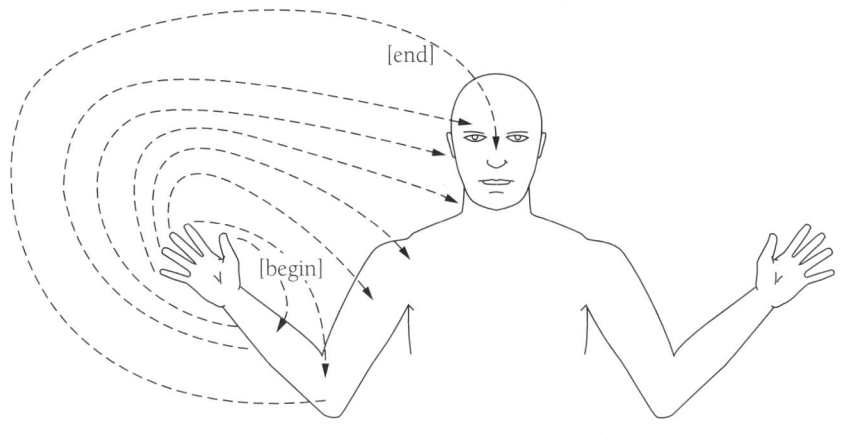

Figure 2.5. The Microgenesis of a Double-Enumeration Procedure

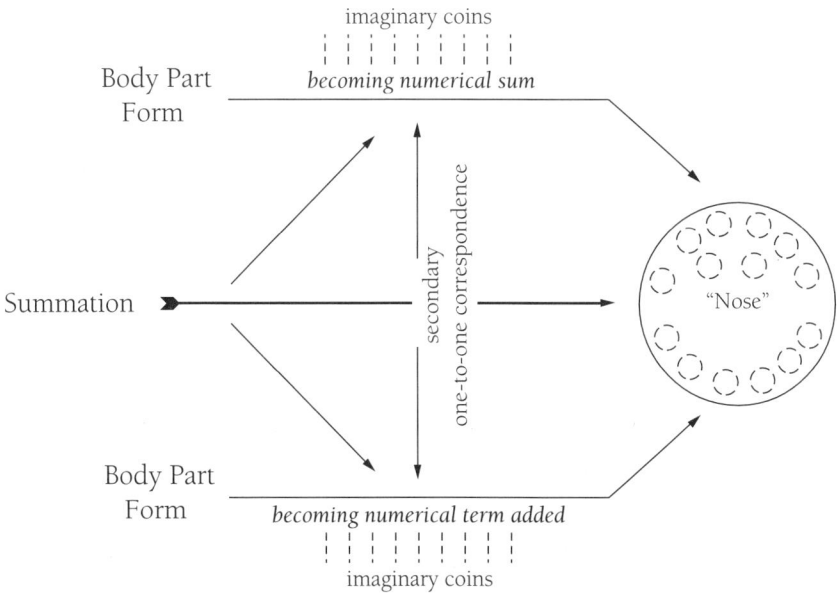

Figure 2.6. The Body-Part Substitution Procedure

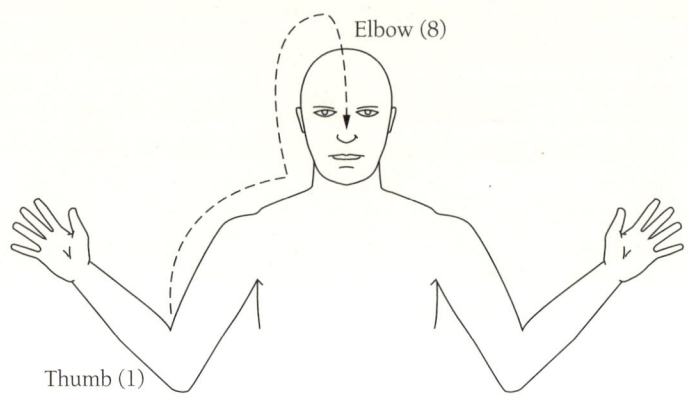

procedure, with one major exception. Rather than establishing physical one-to-one correspondence between two series of body parts, one series is strictly verbal and the other physical. As a consequence, the individual often produces calculations at a quicker pace. Thus, to add six plus eight, an individual may recite the series thumb (1) to inner elbow (8) while pointing to the series forearm (7) to nose (14). Noteworthy here is that body parts are called by the names of other body parts in this strategy to serve the function of keeping track.

Finally, the halved-body procedure (depicted in Figure 2.7) is the most complex strategy observed. In this procedure, rather than using a subseries of the body-part sequence to keep track of a progressive summation of coins, an individual uses each half of the body as a separate register for numerical values. To accomplish this, an individual organizes each half of the body around a focal point such as the shoulder (10). Each arm is then used as an independent register to add or subtract coins. For instance, to add six plus eight coins (Figure 2.7), an individual would "put" eight on one arm (inner elbow) and six on the other (wrist). The addition would be accomplished by a simple transfer of the sixth (wrist) and fifth (little finger) body parts from the first arm to the ninth (biceps) and tenth (shoulder) body parts of the second arm. Thus, the solution would be shoulder (10) and ring finger (4), or 1 kina and 40 toea.

Figure 2.8 shows a frequency distribution of individuals' strategy use for an addition problem as a function of population group. (Due to design considerations described in a prior article [Saxe, 1982], about half of the individuals in each population group solved six plus eight, and the other half solved six

Figure 2.7. The Halved-Body Procedure

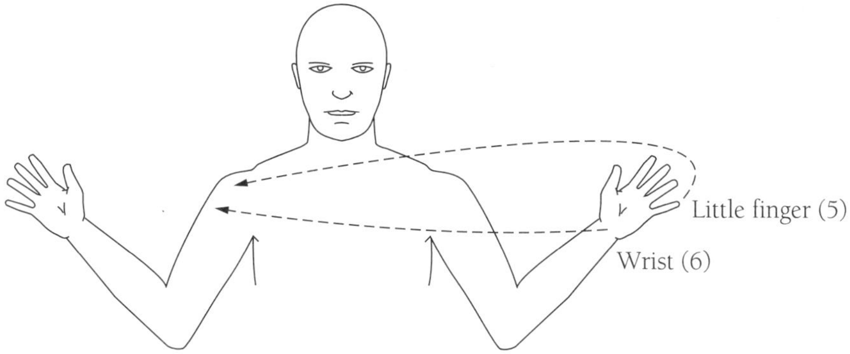

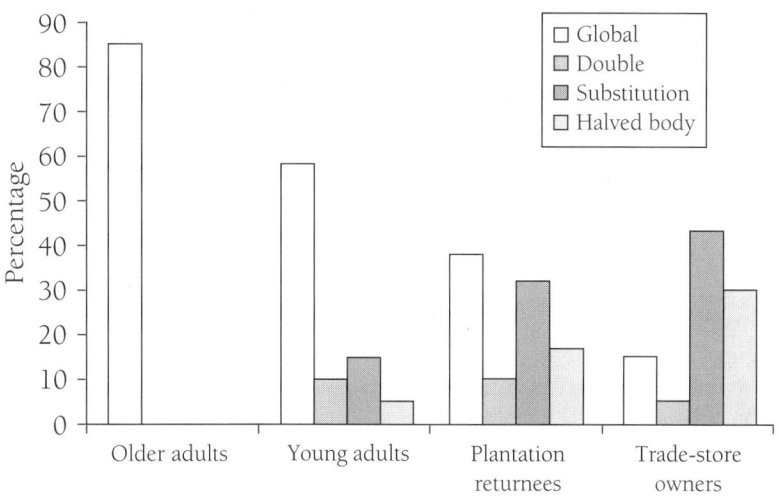

Figure 2.8. Percentage Distribution of Individuals' Solutions to 6 + 8 = ? or 6 + 7 = ? Coin Problems as a Function of Population Group

plus seven. The bar chart contains the pooled strategies for these two problems.) The trend is clear. With greater experience in the money economy, individuals increasingly used strategies that reflect developmentally more sophisticated correspondence operations. Indeed, the vast majority of traditional adults used the global enumeration strategy. With increasing participation in the money economy, individuals used strategies that showed new patterns of schematization reflecting more sophisticated correspondence operations.

In sum, with greater participation in the money economy, body parts were deployed to serve new functions. Those Oksapmin people with only minimal participation in the new economy first attempted to extend the body-counting form to accomplish new arithmetical tasks that emerge in economic transactions. This direct extension from enumerative functions in traditional activities to the new kinds of numerical problems was not adequate to accomplish arithmetical solutions, and it is not even clear that Oksapmin with little experience treated the task as one that involved the cognitive function of arithmetic. Oksapmin with greater experience in the money economy made a labored effort to restructure their prior global counting strategy in such a way that one term was added on to the other (the double-enumeration strategy), creating a new type of body-part to body-part correspondence operation in order to keep track of the addition or subtraction of elements. At more advanced levels in the developmental sequence, we see the body-part-counting form progressively specialized into more sophisticated cognitive forms that serve distinctly arithmetical functions. Now individuals, rather than establishing physical correspondences between body parts as they did previously, efficiently used the name of one body part to refer to another in a body-part substitution strategy. Cognitive forms that were distinctively specialized to serve arithmetical and not enumerative functions were more frequently displayed by trade store owners, who had the most experience with problems of arithmetic that emerge in economic transactions with currency. In their strategies, some trade store owners incorporated a base-ten system linked to the currency as an aid in computation.

Sociogenesis. Up to this point, I have only alluded to the collective aspects of practices of economic exchange and the emergence of collective forms of representation and problem solving. In collective activities, such as exchanges at Oksapmin trade stores, individuals are engaged with microgenetic constructions in communications about quantity and in accomplishing quantity-related problems. Such occasions provide opportunities for reciprocally appropriating features of one another's constructions. In such appropriations, new forms are born as particular representations become valued and institutionalized as regularized ways of representing and accomplishing problems linked to collective practices. The process of diffusion and institutionalization of individuals' microgenetic constructions into the activities of others constitutes a sociogenesis of knowledge.

One product of such a sociogenetic process is a newly emerging structure of the Oksapmin body counting system. In their fieldwork, Moylan and Guilford (personal communication, 1980) noted that many individuals who had considerable experience with the money economy were using a hybrid structure of the Oksapmin body system in their quantitative representations of currency, a development that I found in my own interviews with people with greater experience with economic exchange. The adaptation is one that incorporates the base structure of the early Australian currency system into the indigenous system (depicted in Figure 2.9). With the adapted system, rather

Figure 2.9. The "Hybrid" Oksapmin Number System

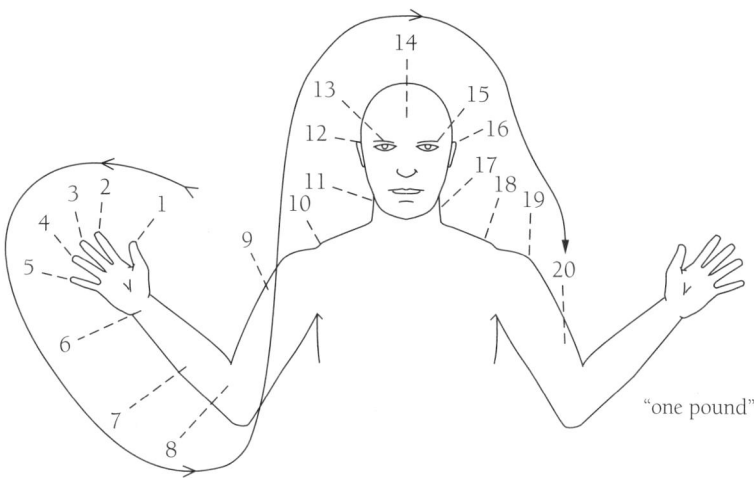

than using all twenty-seven body parts in an enumeration, an individual counts shillings up to the inner elbow on the other side of the body (20) and calls it one round, or 1 pound (reflecting the organization of the first Australian currency system). If the individual needs to continue the count, he or she begins again at the thumb (1) of the first hand (rather than progressing on to the wrist, 21). Similarly, an individual may count 2-kina notes and thus count 40 kina (twenty 2-kina notes equal 40 kina) as one round.

The adapted system, then, has a structure that reflects the base structure of the early Australian currency system but nevertheless is an outgrowth of the standard indigenous system. Those Oksapmin who use this system use it flexibly. There are many ways of expressing the same value, either through combinations of the traditional and the adapted system or through using only one system.

Of course, there are different possible ways of accounting for the emergence of such representational forms in the social history of the Oksapmin community, and diffusion is only one possibility. It may be that the novel collective form of representation (as well as the more sophisticated arithmetical strategies) were the products of independent invention and not diffusion. The failings of the indigenous system when dealing with the emerging problems of economic exchange with great numbers associated with currency would support this view, as many individuals were dealing with problems of representing great values under the constraints of Oksapmin body-part numeration. Although independent invention may certainly play a role in the construction of new representational forms, the press for communication between individuals certainly points to the importance of diffusion and institutionalization as core sociogenetic processes in accounts of the interplay between culture and development.

A Further Application of the Framework

The recent history of arithmetic in the Oksapmin community presents a case in which the interplay between microgenetic, ontogenetic, and sociogenetic processes is remarkably apparent in everyday practices. The account of development sketched here can serve as a useful starting point for understanding the interplay between cultural practices and developmental processes not only in entire societies like the Oksapmin but also in very small scale communities, such as classrooms in today's schools. To conclude, I illustrate with observations of an upper elementary mathematics classroom made as a part of a larger research project (Gearhart and others, forthcoming; Saxe, Gearhart, and Seltzer, forthcoming; Stipek and others, 1998).

The teacher, Ms. Snow, was working in her fourth-grade classroom with a mathematics curriculum unit on fractions. The unit supported students' mathematical inquiry and joint work. A core mathematical concept targeted in the unit was that fractions are not defined by their appearance (for example, a semicircle as "one-half" or a quarter of a circle as "one-fourth"); rather, a fraction is defined by a relation between parts and wholes (for example, a whole partitioned into four equivalent parts creates four fourths, regardless of their shape, and the four fourths are equivalent to the whole). In one of the early activities supported by the unit, students were working at their desks with copies of a square composed of dots defining sixteen cells (see Figure 2.10a). The teacher asked the students to show many different ways of creating "one-half" using the larger square. Later, she introduced problems of creating many ways to show one-fourth, one-eighth, and then one-sixteenth. In the final activity, children were asked to create and show squares depicting different fractions that were later to be assembled in a class quilt (one student's drawing is depicted in Figure 2.10b).*

Let us consider how analyses of microgenesis, ontogenesis, and sociogenesis sketched in the Oksapmin case apply to developing understandings of fractions in Ms. Snow's classroom.

Microgenesis. For children to create mathematical representations with fraction words (forms) in the partitioning activity, they must engage in a microgenetic construction (just like the Oksapmin when they used body parts to represent cardinal numbers). Like the Oksapmin case, the microgenesis involves a threefold schematization of a representational vehicle (in this case, fraction words), a representational object (in this case, part-whole relations between cells and the entire square), and a schematization between vehicle and object such that the vehicle (fraction word) comes to stand for the object (relations between parts and wholes). Thus, a child might shade squares, conceptualizing "one-fourth" as a representational vehicle to stand for the relation between parts (four squares) and whole (sixteen squares).

---

*Tom Bennett and I had the good fortune of being regular visitors to Ms. Snow's classroom, Tom making observations and providing some assistance on a regular basis. It was Tom's visits and classroom support that enabled our analysis.

Figure 2.10a. Sixteen-Cell Worksheet Presented to Students

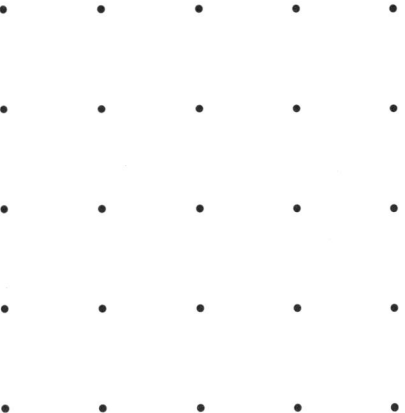

Figure 2.10b. Child's Creation of Fractional Parts Using the Sixteen-Cell Worksheet

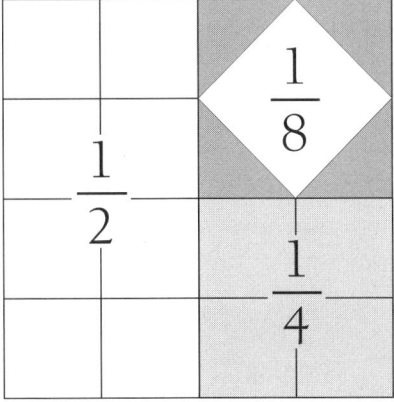

Ontogenesis. Just as in the Oksapmin case, in which there was evidence of form-function shifts in individual development in the accomplishment of numerical problems, observations and interviews with children in Ms. Snow's class showed that children's schematizing activities shift over the course of ontogenesis. Indeed, less mathematically sophisticated children created representational meanings with fraction words that differed qualitatively from more sophisticated children. For example, less sophisticated children tended to schematize fraction words to serve the function of whole-number words. Such children used "one-fourth" to refer to a particular kind of piece (for example, a quartered circle) or a particular number of pieces (for example, four pieces). With increasing participation in partitioning activities, there was a form-function shift. Children began to differentiate and coordinate part-whole relations and began to use fraction terms to serve the function of representing relations between parts and wholes.

Sociogenesis. Finally, we also observed various sociogenetic processes in Ms. Snow's classroom involving the production of new means of accomplishing problems and the spread of these means through the classroom such that they became normative procedures, analogous to aspects of sociogenesis in the Oksapmin. Consider one such case. In their collaborative work, some children had developed an understanding of fractions as relations between parts and wholes. They colored eight cells in different parts of the square to represent one-half (eight of sixteen cells), four cells to represent one-fourth (four of sixteen cells), and two cells to represent one-eighth (two of sixteen cells); subsequently, they abbreviated their analysis of parts and wholes such that they made use of the number of pieces that would be equivalent to each fractional part as they produced different squares. The procedure of counting pieces to create specific fractions was imitated by others and spread through the classroom. For many, eight, four, and two cells became synonymous with the terms *one-half, one-fourth,* and *one-eighth,* respectively. Appreciating that the counting strategy was becoming a classroom norm, Ms. Snow administered an assessment to her class that depicted two squares, one with sixteen and the other with twenty-four cells, both of which had eight cells shaded. She wrote on the problem sheet, "Both squares have eight colored squares, but one shows one-half and the other shows one-third. Explain why." She found many children who were stumped, and targeted those children for additional help, an effort to redirect the process of sociogenesis.

Concluding Remark

In this chapter, I have sketched (1) ways of understanding cognitive development that highlight its cultural roots and (2) ways of understanding cultural change that highlight its roots in individual development. In the account, processes of microgenesis, ontogenesis, and sociogenesis play off of one another in collective cultural practices. In microgenesis, individuals create schematizations that build on prior representational and strategic constructions (ontogenesis). In turn, these schematizations may become appropriated by others, becoming seeds for the spread of new collective forms of representation or procedures for problem solving in a community (sociogenesis). With the sociogenesis of cultural forms, individuals gain access to new forms for microgenetic schematization that become the basis for new ways of engaging in practices and the germs for subsequent ontogenetic shifts in knowledge. Such an account may not only reveal the interplay between cultural and developmental processes over the social history of traditional groups but also provide a frame for understanding the dynamics of cognitive development in collective practices closer to home.

References

Cole, M. *Cultural Psychology: A Once and Future Discipline.* Cambridge, Mass.: Harvard University Press, 1997.

Gearhart, M., and others. "When Can Educational Reforms Make a Difference? Opportunities to Learn Fractions in Elementary Mathematics Classrooms." *Journal for Research in Mathematics Education,* forthcoming.

Lancy, D. F. *Cross-Cultural Studies in Cognition and Mathematics.* Orlando, Fla.: Academic Press, 1983.

Luria, A. R. *Cognitive Development: Its Cultural and Social Foundations.* Cambridge, Mass.: Harvard University Press, 1976.

Piaget, J. "Piaget's Theory." In P. H. Mussen (ed.), *Carmichael's Manual of Child Psychology.* New York: Wiley, 1970.

Saxe, G. B. "Developing Forms of Arithmetic Operations Among the Oksapmin of Papua New Guinea." *Developmental Psychology,* 1982, *18,* 583–594.

Saxe, G. B., Gearhart, M., and Seltzer, M. "Relations Between Classroom Practices and Students' Developing Mathematical Understandings." *Cognition and Instruction,* forthcoming.

Scribner, S. "Vygotsky's Uses of History." In J. V. Wertsch (ed.), *Culture, Communication, and Cognition: Vygotskian Perspectives.* New York: Cambridge University Press, 1985.

Scribner, S., and Cole, M. *The Psychology of Literacy.* Cambridge, Mass.: Harvard University Press, 1981.

Stipek, D. J., and others. "The Value (and Convergence) of Practices Suggested by Motivation Research and Promoted by Mathematics Education Reformers." *Journal for Research in Mathematics Education,* 1998, *29,* 465–488.

Vygotsky, L. *Mind in Society* (M. Cole, V. John-Steiner, S. Scribner, and E. Souberman, eds.). Cambridge, Mass.: Harvard University Press, 1978.

Vygotsky, L. *Thought and Language* (A. Kozulin, ed.). Cambridge, Mass.: MIT Press, 1986.

Werner, H., and Kaplan, B. *Symbol Formation.* New York: Wiley, 1962.

Wertsch, J. *Voices of the Mind.* Cambridge, Mass.: Harvard University Press, 1991.

GEOFFREY B. SAXE is professor of education at the University of California, Berkeley.

Through the longitudinal study of families over two decades in Chiapas, Mexico, this chapter relates historical changes on the macro level to changes in human development and socialization on the micro level.

Cultural Change and Human Development

Patricia M. Greenfield

Cross-cultural studies of cognitive development preceded studies of cultural learning. The former studies made an implicit assumption that *culture is external whereas development is internal.* Bruner's cultural psychology (1990) and Tomasello, Kruger, and Ratner's cultural learning (1993) assume, by contrast, that culture is *inside* the individual, that human beings are intrinsically social and primed both to learn from and to teach their conspecifics. With this new assumption, the old dichotomy between biology as nature and culture as nurture breaks down. Culture becomes part of human nature. Most important for present purposes, the conception of culture as internal rather than external privileges the study of developmental processes of cultural appropriation, to use a term originated by Saxe (1991). But studies of intergenerational cultural apprenticeship (Rogoff, 1990)

An earlier version of this chapter was presented at Development, Evolution, and Culture, an invited symposium organized by Elliot Turiel at the twenty-fifth annual symposium of the Jean Piaget Society, Berkeley, Calif., June 1, 1995, and at the Growing Mind, Geneva, Sept. 1996. Thanks to Emily Yut and the Thursday lab group for discussion and feedback on a previous version of this chapter. Special appreciation to Leslie Devereaux for help in the field and help in understanding Zinacantec culture and people. Thanks to Ashley Maynard for help with the video illustrations and the manuscript. Deep gratitude to Carla Childs and the late Shun Pavlu for being part of it all.

The research on which this paper is based was supported by the Spencer Foundation, the National Geographic Society, the UCLA Latin American Center, the UCLA Center for the Study of Women, the National Institutes of Health Fogarty International Center, the Minority International Research Training Program to UCLA—El Colegio de la Frontera Sur (TW00061), El Colegio de la Frontera Sur, the UCLA Academic Senate, the Harvard Center for Cognitive Studies, the Bunting Institute of Radcliffe College, and the Milton Fund of Harvard Medical School.

must not merely elucidate the learning processes by which cultural skills are *transmitted* from an older to a younger generation. They must also elucidate the learning processes by which cultural skills are *transformed* from one generation to the next. This is the psychological issue of cultural change, raised by Wolfgang Edelstein in Chapter One and Geoffrey Saxe in Chapter Two of this volume.

Cross-Cultural Comparison: Indirect Methods for Studying Cultural Change and Human Development

The earliest methods for addressing cultural change from a psychological perspective were *cross-cultural* comparative studies of cognitive skills, at first based on the crude and simplistic notion of a ladder of cultural evolution. Later studies used methodologically tighter *within-culture* comparative methods to assess the impact of locally observed cultural changes on cognitive processes and cognitive development: Saxe's study of the impact of commercial development on Oksapmin number concepts in New Guinea (1982), Vygotsky and Luria's study of the effect of collectivization on logical operations in the Soviet Union (Luria, 1976), and my study of the effect of schooling on the development of categorization and conservation in Senegal (Greenfield, 1966; Greenfield, Reich, and Olver, 1966) are examples of cross-sectional studies that make inferences concerning the effects of longitudinal sociocultural change.

However, cross-sectional studies can produce only *indirect* evidence concerning cultural change. This is because one must assume that the diachronic or longitudinal effect of the variable under study is the same as the synchronic or cross-sectional effect: for example, that Luria's collectivized peasants in Uzbekistan *used to* think like their uncollectivized neighbors before collectivization took place.

However, when researchers address historical change by comparing two contemporaneous human groups, it is always a possibility that *both* groups being compared have changed during the historical process under study. In Luria's study, for example, both uncollectivized and collectivized peasants may have changed during the postrevolutionary period of collectivization. Even more problematic, there is always a possibility of differential selection bias in the two groups being compared: for example, collectivized and uncollectivized peasants may well have been different before collectivization took place. Consequently there is a need for direct, longitudinal study of historical change.

Cross-Generational Comparison: A Direct Method for Studying Cultural Change and Human Development

I would now like to describe a unique research design that is both historical and longitudinal: it compares socialization and development in two successive generations of the same group of families. The study of the second generation was begun two decades after the study of the first generation had been completed. This research project explores the relations between sociohistorical transformations and human development in a direct way, by following a group of families over two generations—studying their learning and representational processes before and after processes of important ecological change. More specifically, we have investigated the historical transition from agriculture to commerce, focusing on its developmental and learning implications. The study site is a community in transition from agricultural subsistence to commercial entrepreneurship and cash.

Our study examines the relationship between intergenerational continuity and intergenerational change on the cultural level and processes of learning, innovation, and cognitive development on the individual level. In so doing, we elucidate the role of both social interaction and external representational tools in these processes of cultural continuity and change.

Theoretical Framework and Questions

My major theoretical proposition is that as cultures change over historical time, the very processes of cultural learning and cultural transmission also change. More specifically, a somewhat different set of learning processes are highlighted when cultures are in a more stable state, compared with when they are in a more dynamic state. A second theoretical proposition is that even in periods of cultural change, some learning processes of the individual and some cultural foundations of the group remain constant. A third theoretical proposition is that cultural change on the economic level leads to changes in representational strategies on the cognitive level (compare Saxe, 1982).

Insofar as the process of socialization prepares the next generation to participate in society, the process and its outcomes should change when the conditions faced by that next generation differ from the environment in which their parents grew up. Socialization is intrinsically future-oriented: it prepares children for an adulthood that still lies in the future. However, a key question is, in conditions of change, do parents merely recreate the apprenticeship process that they underwent as children? Or do parents have the capacity to develop new methods and processes of apprenticeship as societal conditions—in this case, economic conditions—change? And what, if any, are the consequences of such changes for the development of their children?

At the same time, as the cultural historical school emphasizes (for example, Scribner, 1985), there is an accumulation of cultural history; there is always continuity as well as change. This continuity provides a foundation that persists and affects processes of learning and representation through the course of sociohistorical change.

In human history, there have been three major ecological adaptations: hunting and gathering, agriculture, and commerce, which includes emphasis on advanced technology. It is hypothesized that each ecology emphasizes a different set of skills, different developmental pathways, and different processes of socialization or cultural transmission.

The First Generation

In 1969 and 1970, in collaboration with Carla Childs, I carried out a number of studies of culture, learning, and cognitive development in Nabenchauk, a hamlet of the agrarian Maya community of Zinacantan (summarized in Greenfield, Brazelton, and Childs, 1989, and Greenfield and Childs, 1991). Zinacantan is a Tzotzil-speaking community, located in the highlands of Chiapas, Mexico (Vogt, [1970] 1990). All communication between researchers and subjects occurred in Tzotzil.

Our focus was on the cognitive skills and learning processes involved in the important cultural technology of weaving, the most complex skill in the culture, a skill acquired by all Zinacantec women (Childs and Greenfield, 1980; Greenfield, 1984; Greenfield and Childs, 1977). Weaving was our focus for studying processes of informal education, learning, and cognition in a society in which education does not traditionally take place in school (Greenfield and Lave, 1982). Weaving is considered to be the essence of Zinacantec womanhood. Figure 3.1 shows a girl seated at the ancient Maya backstrap loom.

Schooling was not entirely absent from the community, although it was an outside force, carried out in a foreign language, Spanish, and delivered by teachers who were Ladinos, a local term for people who identify with national Mexican culture and are often racially mixed (mestizo) between indigenous Maya and Spanish. There were two elementary schools in the village, attended almost exclusively by boys. No one in the community had an education

Figure 3.1. Katal Pavlu Seated at a Backstrap Loom, 1970

Source: © Sheldon Greenfield.

beyond the elementary school level. Many who began school left before completing sixth grade.

Artifacts. Woven artifacts, like other parts of the culture, were stable and little changing, defined by tradition. The discipline of anthropology has called attention to the dangers of assuming stability in a culture up to the moment of the investigator's entrance. However, I had an opportunity to check empirically the hypothesis of relative stability in the traditions of woven patterns before my arrival in 1969. I was given access to a collection of ritual textiles created and used by the Vasquez family in Nabenchauk. This collection went from the 1940s into the 1980s; it confirmed the slow pace of change and, more important, the relative uniformity of textile designs up through 1969–1970, the point at which we studied the first generation.

In that period, woven patterns were limited to two red-and-white striped configurations, one multicolor stripe, and one gray-and-white basketweave pattern. Figure 3.2 shows the two red-and-white striped patterns, with two variants of each pattern.

Cultural Learning. Based on our research in 1969 and 1970, we concluded that the goal of Zinacantec education and socialization was the intergenerational replication of tradition: learning to weave meant learning to weave a few very specific patterns. According to the findings from our videotaped observations, the particular way in which weaving was taught fostered this goal: the learning process was a relatively error-free one, in which the teacher, usually the mother, sensitively provided help, models for observation, and verbal direction in accord with the developmental level of the learner (Childs and Greenfield, 1980; Greenfield, 1984). Mother provided a scaffold of help that allowed the learner to complete a weaving she could not have done by herself. Figure 3.3 shows a mother helping her nine-year-old daughter, Katal, to weave. The image of four hands on the loom was a paradigmatic symbol for weaving apprenticeship in 1970.

This scene is in sharp contrast to what occurred two decades later when Katal's daughter, also age nine, learned to weave in 1991.

Because the 1970 version of the apprenticeship process was highly structured by the older generation and did not allow room for learner experimentation and discovery, the method of informal education (or apprenticeship) was well adapted for the continuation of tradition, the maintenance of the status quo.

Cognitive Representation. In 1969 and 1970, we did a cognitive experiment (Greenfield and Childs, 1977). One of its goals was to assess the cognitive effects of weaving on pattern representation. Sticks placed in a frame were used to represent striped patterns (see Figure 3.4). Note that in addition to being various colors, the sticks came in three widths: thin, medium, and broad.

At the outset of the experiment, each subject was asked to create representations of two traditional Zinacantec woven patterns. These were the same patterns shown in Figure 3.2. The top pattern in Figure 3.2 was used for the male poncho, worn by the subject at the left side of Figure 3.4. The bottom pattern in Figure 3.2 is used for the female shawl, worn by the experimenter, Carla

Figure 3.2. Two Red-and-White Striped Woven Patterns, 1969

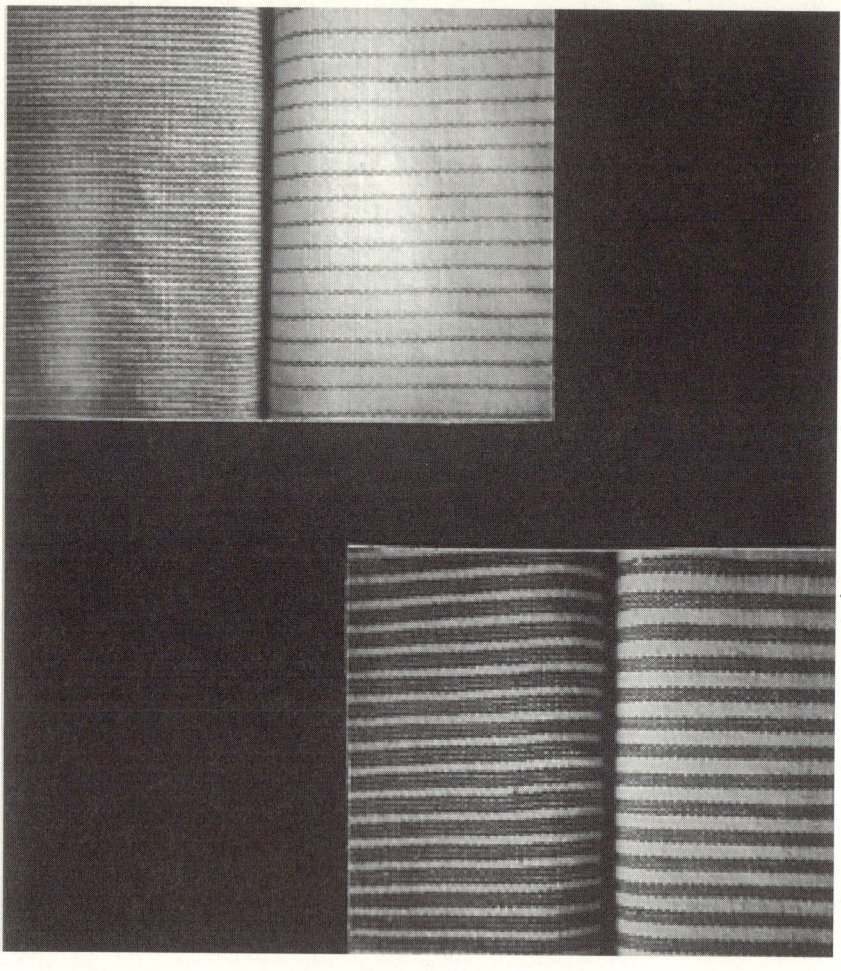

Source: © Carla Childs.

The top pair are two variants of a pattern for a poncho worn by all boys and men. In all variants of the poncho pattern, the basic configuration of alternating thin red and thicker white stripes remains constant. The bottom pair are two variants of a pattern for a shawl worn by all girls and women. In all variants of the shawl pattern, the basic configuration of alternating a complex stripe (three thin reds separated by two thin whites) with a simple white stripe is maintained. Dark stripes represent red in the black-and-white photograph.

Figure 3.3. Xunica Kasya Helping Her Nine-Year-Old Daughter, Katal, with Her Weaving, 1970

Source: Video still, 1970.

Childs, seated to the right in Figure 3.4. It is important to note that the poncho pattern (top of Figure 3.2) is a simple alternation of thin red and thicker white stripes, whereas the shawl pattern (bottom of Figure 3.2) has a complex red stripe consisting of three thin red stripes separated by two thin white ones; this complex red stripe alternates with a white stripe. Other patterns, starting with simple and familiar and progressing toward patterns of increasing complexity and novelty, were then modeled for the subjects to complete in the same frame.

The development of representational strategies moved from simple to complex with increasing age (Greenfield and Childs, 1977). By the time subjects reached teenage years, there was a differentiation of strategies for representing the woven patterns between schooled and unschooled subjects (all male) and between unschooled weavers (female) and nonweavers (male). Figure 3.5 shows a strategy of representation that was used more frequently by teenagers who either wove or had been to school; it was used less frequently by teenagers who had never been to school. We called the strategy depicted in Figure 3.5 a *detailed analytic* or *thread-by-thread analytic* representation. It accurately maintains the distinct configurations of the two striped patterns shown at the top and the bottom of Figure 3.2.

In contrast, unschooled teenage boys used more global, less analytic strategies for representing the woven patterns. Specifically, their strategies less

Figure 3.4. Pattern Representation Experiment

Note: The sticks come in three widths. The subject is seated to the left; the tester, Carla Childs, is to the right.
Source: © Sheldon Greenfield.

frequently indicated analysis of the complexity of the stripe in the shawl (narrow red, narrow white, narrow red, narrow white, narrow red, broad white; see bottom of Figure 3.2); some unschooled teenagers, for example, represented the shawl as a simple alternation of a broad red and a narrow white stripe.

At the same time, note, in Figure 3.5, that broad stripes are represented by grouping thin sticks together, just as, in a weaving, a broad stripe would consist of a series of threads grouped together. Clearly a weaver would know how a pattern was constructed, thread by thread. However, elementary level schooling clearly also pushed subjects in the direction of a more analytic approach to representing the patterns, including the thread-by-thread detail.

Figure 3.6 shows a technique of representation virtually never used by any Zinacantec subjects in our sample but frequently used by U.S. college students (Greenfield and Childs, 1977).

We called this the *abstract analytic* mode of representation. Like many of the skilled Zinacantec weavers and schooled Zinacantec teenage boys, most U.S. college students maintained the distinct configuration of each pattern, including analysis of the complex stripe in the shawl (right side of Figure 3.6). However, unlike the Zinacantec subjects, they used broad sticks to represent

CULTURAL CHANGE AND HUMAN DEVELOPMENT   45

Figure 3.5. Detailed Analytic Representation of the Two Red-and-White Striped Woven Patterns, 1969

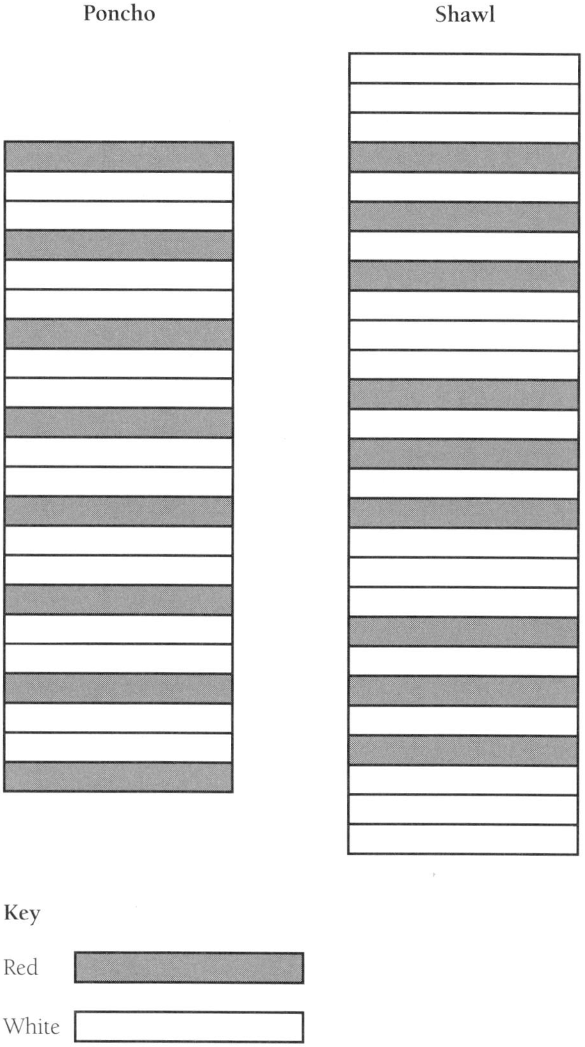

Poncho   Shawl

Key

Red
White

Note: The pattern for the poncho worn by boys and men is shown at the left; it is a representation of the pattern shown at the top of Figure 3.2. The pattern for the shawl worn by girls and women is shown at the right; it is a representation of the pattern shown at the bottom of Figure 3.2.

46 DEVELOPMENT AND CULTURAL CHANGE

Figure 3.6. Abstract Analytic Representation of the Two Red-and-White Striped Woven Patterns

Note: The pattern for the poncho worn by boys and men is represented at the left; it is a representation of the pattern shown at the top of Figure 3.2. The pattern for the shawl worn by girls and women is represented at the right; it is a representation of the pattern shown at the bottom of Figure 3.2.

broad stripes (poncho and shawl representations in Figure 3.6). This strategy is abstract in that the representation of the broad stripe eliminates the detail of the thread-by-thread strategy.

Whereas both weaving and elementary level schooling were associated with the detailed analytic strategy, advanced education or other distinctive features of U.S. culture were associated with the abstract mode of analysis. One possible causal factor in the prevalence of the abstract mode of representation is the importance of money, as an abstract medium of exchange, in the U.S. economy. The abstraction of money contrasts with the specificity of barter exchanges, common in subsistence cultures like Zinacantan. This question of causal factors for the abstract analytic mode of pattern representation was pursued through the historical replication of the experiment two decades later; its results will be discussed in the last section of this chapter.

Symbolic Tools. These we define as tools for creating external representations. This was not an area of study in 1969 and 1970 because there were virtually no tools for creating external representations in the community. The only exception was the winding board that could be used to create a striped warp for the striped or basketweave textiles that could be copied by other weavers. Although there were statues of saints in the churches, these were brought in from outside the community, so no representational tools for creating them existed. One did not see paper and pencil in homes. Nor did one see figurative drawing. The area of symbolic tools came to our attention in the follow-up study two decades later because the situation in this arena had changed so drastically.

Ecological Change: The Next Generation

Seventeen years after we completed our original field research in Zinacantan, I heard about a major social and economic change (Cancian, 1987, 1990, 1992). Men who formerly farmed now were in the transport business. They had become commercial entrepreneurs, running a van service back and forth to the neighboring Mexican city of San Cristobal de las Casas. Others had entered the trucking business as both drivers and owners.

We investigated the implications of this ecological and economic transformation for change in each of the four areas introduced earlier:

1. Change in artifacts and the skills that produce them
2. Changes in processes of cultural learning and cultural transmission
3. Changes in modes of cognitive representation
4. Changes in symbolic tools

In 1991, I returned to the community with my original collaborator, Carla Childs; Leslie Devereaux, an anthropologist with years of experience in the community, and my daughter, Lauren Greenfield, a photographer with an assignment from the National Geographic Society, also accompanied us. Our research goal was to investigate the changes by replicating our studies with the next generation, now roughly the same age as their parents, aunts, and uncles had been when they served as subjects in the 1969 and 1970 studies.

We made certain predictions about the nature of changes that we thought we would find. Each prediction was made strictly on theoretical grounds (for example, Greenfield and Lave, 1982). Neither Carla Childs nor I had been back to the community to observe what was going on since 1970.

As we explored change, we also noted the foundation of constancy provided by the accumulation of history in each of the four areas. Each of these areas—artifacts, modes of cultural learning, development of modes of representation, and symbolic tools—will now be taken up and elaborated, one at a time.

Artifacts. Because entrepreneurship entails an ideology of innovation, I predicted that innovation would enter the culture in a general way, affecting many areas of life. One such area was textile and clothing production. Therefore, I predicted that woven textiles would no longer be limited to a small stock of patterns; instead, weavers would constantly innovate new patterns. This was conceptualized as a major shift in representational processes and therefore as a shift in cognitive development. The new array of patterns would also constitute a shift in the stock of cultural artifacts.

The results were quite astonishing. A tremendous amount of innovation was taking place in woven patterns. Some of the innovation was connected to the spread of commercialization to weaving production: new items had been developed to sell to tourists. But the innovation in the clothing Zinacantecs wove for themselves was even greater. The contrast with the single pattern for each article of clothing found in the earlier period was great. Figure 3.7 shows two brothers dressed in identical ponchos. Indeed, all males wore the same poncho in 1969 and 1970.

By 1991, each poncho was different. Two examples are shown in Figures 3.8a and 3.8b.

These examples include innovation in both the weaving (the brocaded bands at the bottom of each poncho) and the embroidery (the vertically arranged designs above the bottom border, shown more completely in Figure 3.8a).

Similar changes had occurred in girls' and women's blouses. Figure 3.9 shows the standard blouse in 1969 and 1970.

Figures 3.10a and 3.10b show two variants of a potentially infinite number of different embroidered patterns.

As these examples suggest, our prediction was confirmed: Zinacantecs of the 1990s were engaging in a constant process of pattern creation. No two pieces of clothing or other woven items were exactly alike. The results were the same in the domain of embroidery. We saw both new motifs and new recombinations of old motifs. Geometric designs (as in Figure 3.10a) had greatly expanded, and figurative representations (as in Figure 3.10b) had arrived; there had been no figurative representation in Zinacantan two decades earlier.

Figure 3.7. Two Zinacantec Brothers, Marian and Antun Pavlu, Dressed in Ponchos Using the Woven Stripe Shown in Figure 3.2, Standard in 1969 and 1970

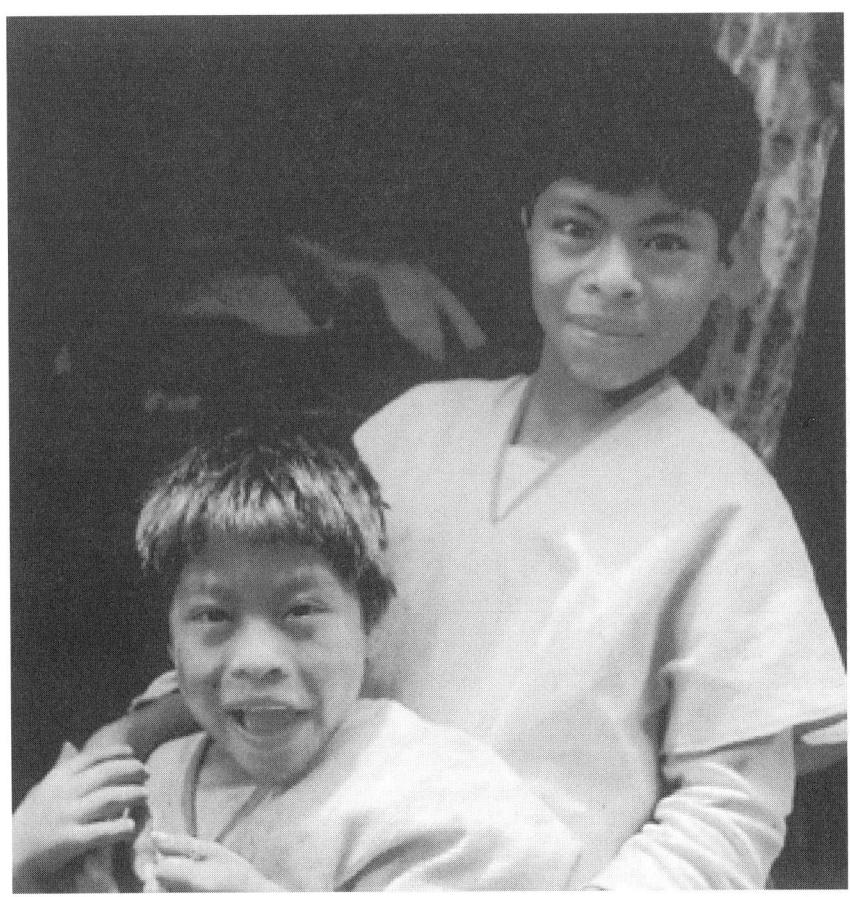

Source: © Sheldon Greenfield.

Note, however, that there is cultural constancy in change: for example, the style and background stripe of the men's poncho remained the same. The simple red-and-white stripe shown at the top of Figure 3.2 was still the background pattern for the ponchos shown in Figures 3.8a and 3.8b, even though the stripe now had more red than white. The cut of the old blouse in Figure 3.9 had not changed in the new blouses (Figures 3.10a and 3.10b). Similarly, the positioning of the embroidery around the neck and running down from each shoulder had stayed the same; the embroidery had simply become much more elaborate and variable.

Modes of Cultural Learning. Based mainly on our earlier research and on observing a backstrap weaving class in Cambridge, Massachusetts, I had

Figures 3.8a and 3.8b. Variants of the Poncho Worn by Boys and Men, 1991

Source: © Lauren Greenfield.

Figure 3.9. Example of Zinacantec Blouse, Worn by Katal Pavlu, That Was Standard in 1969 and 1970

Source: © Sheldon Greenfield.

developed a theory centering on a contrast between the goals of two methods of informal education: scaffolding with observational models (which was typical in 1970 and which was illustrated in Figure 3.3) and relatively independent trial-and-error or discovery learning (Greenfield and Lave, 1982). In a sense, as Gelman (personal communication, 1991) has pointed out, we predicted a historical shift from a Vygotskian model of learning (emphasizing scaffolded guidance) to a Piagetian model (emphasizing independent discovery).

Whereas the first model, according to my theory, is adapted to transmitting a tradition intact, the second, with its emphasis on the learner's own discovery process, is adapted to the development of an ability to innovate. If innovation had in fact entered the culture as a value orientation in response to or as part of commercial entrepreneurship, I thought that weaving education would make a corresponding shift. Earlier the teacher had carefully built a scaffold of help for the learner, providing help before the learner had an opportunity to make a serious error. Because the learner, in this situation, received very

Figure 3.10a and 3.10b Variants of the Zinacantec Blouse, 1991

Source: © Lauren Greenfield.

CULTURAL CHANGE AND HUMAN DEVELOPMENT   53

little opportunity to make a mistake, let alone to explore, I predicted that as the economy became more entrepreneurial, the methods of teaching and learning would change to a more independent trial-and-error approach, an approach that allows room for discovery.

Did the predicted change occur? A well-controlled historical comparison provides important information. The girl learning to weave in Figure 3.3 grew up and had five daughters of her own. In 1991, one of the daughters, Loxa, was the same age (nine) that her mother, Katal Pavlu, had been when we videotaped her learning to weave twenty-one years earlier.

The nature of Loxa's apprenticeship in 1991 was completely different from that of her mother in 1970. First of all, the generation of the teacher had changed. Instead of teaching her daughter herself, as her mother had done for her (Figure 3.3), Katal assigned her twelve- or thirteen-year-old daughter, Xunka, to serve as Loxa's teacher (Figure 3.11).

Second, in contrast to the way in which her mother anticipated her daughter's need for help, Xunka paid little attention to her younger sister as she sat working at the loom. Note, in Figure 3.11, that Xunka's visual attention is not on her younger sister, seated at the loom. Indeed, in one segment of the videotaped weaving session, Loxa (the learner) had to call her sister twice to get her attention and ask for help. The help is forthcoming; the difference from a generation earlier is that it is learner- rather than teacher-initiated.

Figure 3.11. Weaving Learner Loxa Santis, Age Nine, and Her Teacher, Her Older Sister Xunka

Source: Video still, 1991.

A comparison of Figure 3.3 and Figure 3.11 shows another related difference: the 1991 teacher in Figure 3.11 is much more distant from the learner than is the 1970 teacher in Figure 3.3. Third, Katal reported that her daughters had started to weave on their own initiative, whereas she had begun in response to the directive of her mother. All of these differences are indices of a historical shift from a more interdependent to a more independent learning process (see Greenfield, 1994).

In summary, changes in the material culture of woven and embroidered artifacts to an innovative mode entailed change in the method by which weaving was taught and learned. The mode of cultural learning changed from a closely guided one, adapted to maintaining an unchanging stock of traditional artifacts, to a more independent one, adapted to creating cultural innovation and novelty. Quantitative analysis indicated that this historical change in methods of apprenticeship was a general one, not limited to the particular historical case study presented here (Greenfield, Maynard, and Childs, 1997).

Through the changes, there were also some constants in this process. Just as the woven artifacts themselves mixed tradition and innovation, many parts of the acquisition process had constant as well as novel elements. One constant element was a preweaving stage of play weaving on a toy loom (Figure 3.12).

Figure 3.12. Loxa Pavlu, Age Five, Creating a Play Weaving at Her Toy Loom, 1991

Source: © Lauren Greenfield.

This was an experience reported by virtually all learners and their mothers. The toy loom (see Figure 3.12) is a culturally standardized tool that, because of its slightly different design from the real loom, is easier to set up (Greenfield, forthcoming). Its constancy over time illustrates how cultural history builds on the past, even as it transforms it.

Thus far we have confirmed our first prediction concerning the historical transformation of cultural artifacts and our second prediction concerning the historical transformation of cultural learning. Our third prediction concerns the historical transformation of cognitive processes.

Development of Modes of Representation. Because of the growth of the cash economy, with its abstract medium of monetary exchange, we anticipated that our experimental study of pattern representation would show historical growth in the use of abstract representational strategies as the Zinacantec ecology moved from agriculture to commerce.

Indeed, this is what we found. The abstract analytic way of representing the woven patterns, shown in Figure 3.6, had appeared for the first time in Nabenchauk. In general, abstraction (using thick sticks to represent broad stripes) had significantly increased between 1969–1970 and 1991.

The detailed analytic approach had not disappeared. However, the distribution of representational styles had changed to include the abstract analytic approach. In general, the balance between detailed and abstract representation of the woven patterns had shifted to a lower frequency of detailed (that is, thread-by-thread) representations of the woven stripes. Against a background of historical constancy, the economic transition from agriculture to commerce brought with it a more abstract approach to representing cultural artifacts.

In the final section, I move from the representation of cultural artifacts to the nature of cultural tools.

Symbolic Tools. The final aspect of the results was unpredicted. It relates to the development of new symbolic tools. Although the backstrap loom, of ancient Maya origin, has remained the same, there have been some new symbolic tools that relate specifically to the creation of varied designs. I term these tools *meta-representational* because they are tools for creating patterns, that is, for creating representations. No meta-representational tools had existed in the earlier period.

The most interesting and most complex of these new meta-representational tools is the use of paper patterns for weaving. Figure 3.13 shows a pattern being used for brocade weaving in 1991. The pattern book is not of Zinacantec origin; it was printed in Mexico City.

What is particularly interesting are the representational conventions that were developed for using such patterns for weaving. Because these printed patterns were developed for cross-stitch embroidery, the pattern is printed on a grid of squares; each square represents one cross-stitch on a piece of embroidered fabric.

However, unlike embroidery, weaving is not naturally organized in squares. There are parallel warp (or frame) threads, shown in white in Figure 3.13; and there are parallel weft threads that go over and under the warp threads, at right

Figure 3.13. Pattern Book (Printed in Mexico City) Being Used for Brocade Weaving, 1991

Source: © Lauren Greenfield.

angles to them. (In the figure, the weft are the dark threads in the woven part of the warp, to the left of the unwoven white warp threads.)

Therefore, it was necessary to develop a representational strategy for creating hypothetical squares in order to use the printed patterns for weaving. And this is exactly what Zinacantec weavers did. One weaver told me that one square would correspond to one thread in the warp dimension (white threads) and to four threads in the weft dimension (the darker, crosswise threads). This is a fairly complex representational code to create, especially with just a few years of formal education. Zinacantec girls have appropriated a new symbolic tool, the printed pattern, and transformed it, as part of the process of cultural appropriation (see Chapter Two in this volume).

However, most of the older generation of mothers do not know how to weave with paper patterns; for them, the absence of formal schooling is a barrier to understanding the code of symbolic correspondences (Greenfield and Maynard, 1997). Because of the much higher rate of using paper patterns in the younger generation, we see that innovative cognitive change is concentrated in the younger generation, a phenomenon that is very familiar in our own society.

Historical continuity is manifested in the fact that Zinacantec females, especially members of the younger generation, still use other people's textiles and clothing as tools for creating patterns. The textiles of others are used as models both for the traditional background designs (for example, red and white stripes) and for the newer figurative or geometric designs.

Conclusions

The direct, controlled study of cultural historical change has reaped rich rewards in creating theoretical and empirical links between individual processes of cultural apprenticeship and societal processes of cultural change. It points to a process of reciprocal change in which societal conditions provide an ecological push toward new modes of cultural apprenticeship, as new modes of apprenticeship create a younger generation with the skill profile appropriate to the changed societal conditions. Zinacantec mothers are not bound by the way they were taught weaving as young girls two decades earlier. Instead, they seem to follow the rule put forth by Pérusse, Neale, Heath, and Eaves (1994): teach what is adaptive in the present context.

Our findings confirm my major theoretical proposition that as cultures change over time, the very processes of cultural learning and cultural transmission also change. More specifically, our findings indicate that processes of scaffolded guidance (the processes emphasized by Vygotsky) are highlighted when cultures are in a more stable, tradition-maintaining state. In contrast, processes of independent, trial-and-error experimentation (the processes emphasized by Piaget, [1965] 1977) are highlighted when cultures are in a more dynamic, innovation-oriented state. As the Zinacantecs moved from one state to the other in the space of two decades, the emphasis in their modes of cultural learning changed accordingly.

At the same time, we found continuity in an early stage of weaving apprenticeship, play weaving on the toy loom. This continuity was part of a larger historical continuity in weaving technology, textiles, representational skill, and subsistence lifestyle of the Zinacantecs. Yet points of continuity can become cognitively transformed in the process of cultural change: for example, the historical continuity in the background woven patterns of the men's poncho and women's shawl contrasted with new, more abstract ways of representing these patterns, hypothesized to be a reflection of the intrinsic abstraction of money as a medium of exchange. Historical continuity in the background woven patterns also contrasted with the novelty of the woven and embroidered designs superimposed on this background.

Finally, we observed the appearance of Zinacantan's first meta-representational tools. In this chapter, I have used the example of printed patterns, which function as tools for creating representations. These have been appropriated by the younger, more school-educated generation to support the creation of varied woven and embroidered designs. At the same time, such tools provide external symbolic supports for maintaining and expanding processes of cultural apprenticeship.

In sum, we have observed coordinated changes on the levels of economics, learning modes, artifacts, and cognition. Sociocultural forces on the macro level affected the process of cultural apprenticeship on the micro level. Changes in processes of cultural apprenticeship produced a new generation that was well adapted to the changed ecological niche. In other words, there was a tight relationship between a changing ecological niche and a changing developmental niche (Super and Harkness, 1986).

To end on a speculative note and address one of the themes of this volume, I believe that the changes in cultural apprenticeship, cultural tools, and cognitive modes of representation observed in Nabenchauk are directional. They are directional because world societies are moving in the same direction as the Zinacantecs—toward ever-greater commercialization and commodification. I am much less sure that this direction constitutes progress in the human condition.

References

Bruner, J. "Culture and Human Development: A New Look." *Human Development*, 1990, *33*, 344–355.

Cancian, F. "Proletarianization in Zinacantàn." In M. D. Maclachlan (ed.), *Household Economies and Their Transformations.* Lanham, Md.: University Press of America, 1987.

Cancian, F. "The Zinacantàn Cargo Waiting Lists as a Reflection of Social, Political, and Economic Changes, 1952–1987." In L. Stephen and J. Dow (eds.), *Class, Politics, and Popular Religion in Mexico and Central America.* Washington, D.C.: American Anthropological Association, 1990.

Cancian, F. *The Decline of Community in Zinacantàn: Economy, Public Life, and Social Stratification, 1960–1987.* Stanford, Calif.: Stanford University Press, 1992.

Childs, C. P., and Greenfield, P. M. "Informal Modes of Learning and Teaching: The Case of Zinacanteco Weaving." In N. Warren (ed.), *Studies in Cross-Cultural Psychology.* London: Academic Press, 1980.

Greenfield, P. M. "On Culture and Conservation." In J. S. Bruner and others, *Studies in Cognitive Growth.* New York: Wiley, 1966.

Greenfield, P. M. "A Theory of the Teacher in the Learning Activities of Everyday Life." In B. Rogoff and J. Lave (eds.), *Everyday Cognition: Its Development in Social Context.* Cambridge, Mass.: Harvard University Press, 1984.

Greenfield, P. M. "Independence and Interdependence as Developmental Scripts: Implications for Theory, Research, and Practice." In P. M. Greenfield and R. R. Cocking (eds.), *Cross-Cultural Roots of Minority Child Development.* Mahwah, N.J.: Erlbaum, 1994.

Greenfield, P. M. "Culture and Universals: Integrating Social and Cognitive Development." In L. P. Nucci, G. B. Saxe, and E. Turiel (eds.), *Culture, Thought, and Development.* Mahwah, N.J.: Erlbaum, forthcoming.

Greenfield, P. M., Brazelton, T. B., and Childs, C. P. "From Birth to Maturity in Zinacantan: Ontogenesis in Cultural Context." In V. Bricker and G. Gossen (eds.), *Ethnographic Encounters in Southern Mesoamerica: Celebratory Essays in Honor of Evon Z. Vogt.* Albany: Institute of Mesoamerican Studies, State University of New York, 1989.

Greenfield, P. M., and Childs, C. P. "Weaving, Color Terms, and Pattern Representation: Cultural Influences and Cognitive Development Among the Zinacantecos of Southern Mexico."*Interamerican Journal of Psychology,* 1977, *11,* 23–48.

Greenfield, P. M., and Childs, C. P. "Developmental Continuity in Biocultural Context." In R. Cohen and A. W. Siegel (eds.), *Context and Development.* Mahwah, N.J.: Erlbaum, 1991.

Greenfield, P. M., and Lave, J. "Cognitive Aspects of Informal Education." In D. Wagner and H. Stevenson (eds.), *Cultural Perspectives on Child Development.* New York: Freeman, 1982.

Greenfield, P. M., and Maynard, A. E. "Women, Girls, Apprenticeship, and Schooling: A Longitudinal Study of Historical Change Among the Zinacantecan Maya." Presented at a symposium conducted at the 96th annual meeting of the American Anthropological Association, Washington, D.C., Nov. 1997.

Greenfield, P. M., Maynard, A. E., and Childs, C. P. "History, Culture, Learning, and Development." Presented at the biennial meeting of the Society for Research in Child Development, Apr. 1997.

Greenfield, P. M., Reich, L. C., and Olver, R. R. "On Culture and Equivalence–II." In J. S. Bruner and others, *Studies in Cognitive Growth.* New York: Wiley, 1966.

Luria, A. R. *Cognitive Development: Its Cultural and Social Foundations.* Cambridge, Mass.: Harvard University Press, 1976.

Pérusse, D., Neale, M. C., Heath, A. C., and Eaves, L. J. "Human Parental Behavior: Evidence for Genetic Influence and Potential Implication for Gene-Culture Transmission." *Behavior Genetics,* 1994, *24,* 327–335.

Piaget, J. "Developments in Pedagogy." Reprinted in H. E. Gruber and J. J. Vonèche (eds.), *The Essential Piaget: An Interpretive Reference and Guide.* New York: Basic Books, 1977. (Originally published 1965.)

Rogoff, B. *Apprenticeship in Thinking.* New York: Cambridge University Press, 1990.

Saxe, G. B. "Developing Forms of Arithmetic Operations Among the Oksapmin of Papua New Guinea." *Developmental Psychology,* 1982, *18,* 583–594.

Saxe, G. B. *Culture and Cognitive Development: Studies in Mathematical Understanding.* Mahwah, N.J.: Erlbaum, 1991.

Scribner, S. "Vygotsky's Uses of History." In J. V. Wertsch (ed.), *Culture, Communication, and Cognition: Vygotskian Perspectives.* New York: Cambridge University Press, 1985.

Super, C. M., and Harkness, S. "The Developmental Niche: A Conceptualization at the Interface of Child and Culture." *International Journal of Behavioral Development,* 1986, *9,* 2–25.

Tomasello, M., Kruger, A. C., and Ratner, H. H. "Cultural Learning." *Behavioral and Brain Sciences,* 1993, *16,* 495–552.

Vogt, E. Z. *The Zinacantecos of Mexico: A Modern Maya Way of Life.* Austin, Tex.: Holt, Rinehart and Winston, 1990. (Originally published 1970.)

Vygotsky, L. S. *Mind in Society: The Development of Higher Psychological Processes.* Cambridge, Mass.: Harvard University Press, 1978.

PATRICIA M. GREENFIELD is professor of psychology at the University of California, Los Angeles.

Contrary to their portrayal in the research literature, Japanese preschools exhibit great diversity in terms of teachers' norms and expectations for children as well the type of teaching methods used in the classroom. Three distinct patterns of early schooling are discussed in this chapter, with particular emphasis on preschools that emphasize academic preparation within a large-group context characterized by strict discipline and few opportunities for interaction with peers.

Divergent Cultural Models of Child Rearing and Pedagogy in Japanese Preschools

Susan D. Holloway

Few societies have changed as quickly and radically in the last century as has Japan, yet accounts of current Japanese schools and families are quick to label distinctive patterns as "traditional" without careful analysis of their historical roots. The tendency in writing about Japan is to capture a few images and make claims that they represent the views and practices of the nation. These accounts fail to capture the complexity of this society of more than a hundred million individuals, whose beliefs and actions are patterned by occupation, education, gender, regional affiliation, and other features of their social and physical context. They also fail to uncover the possibility that cultural models of child rearing and education may be conflicting, contested, and resisted by members of the society. Westerners may perceive the relatively placid surface of Japanese society as indicating deep layers of personal contentment and intrasocietal agreement, but a closer look reveals that this is far from true.

There are many reasons why Western writing on Japan has been at once voluminous yet strikingly one-dimensional. Some writers are interested in Japanese practices primarily insofar as they serve the purpose of critiquing the United States (for example, Stevenson and Stigler, 1992). Others attempt to draw macro-level comparisons between Japan and other societies, categorizing Japan along global dimensions such as "group-oriented" or "interdependent" in contrast to the "individualistic" societies of the West (for example, Markus and Kitayama, 1991). Rare indeed are accounts whose primary purpose is to provide a rich description of the everyday lives and thoughts of a segment of Japanese society (see Kondo, 1990, for an example of such an approach).

Japanese education, including the preschool system, has particularly attracted the attention of scholars in the West. However, the literature has failed to document the vitality and diversity of these important socializing institutions. More than 90 percent of children attend at least two years of a licensed preschool or child-care center (Boocock, 1989), reflecting the society's belief that participation in a group experience is essential for enhancing young children's ability to function in Japanese society. At the preschool level, unlike in later years, there is tremendous diversity in the nature of programs available for children. Although licensed preschools must adhere to guidelines set by the Ministry of Education pertaining to teacher training, ratio of students to teacher, equipment, and characteristics of the building and grounds, directors play a very important role in shaping the activities, teaching style, and discipline strategies of their own programs.

Rather than documenting this rich diversity found across Japanese preschools, researchers have focused their attention exclusively on the type of preschool that most Japanese would consider "typical." These preschools have the stated goal of preparing children for life in the social realm (see Hendry, 1986; Lewis, 1995; Peak, 1991; Tobin, Wu, and Davidson, 1989). They provide an opportunity to learn interpersonal skills like empathy (*omoiyari*) through free play. They also introduce children to routine behaviors needed for successful participation in group life, such as greeting the teacher appropriately, managing belongings neatly and efficiently, and fitting into the temporal rhythms of the classroom. Teachers in these society-centered preschools are usually warm, patient, and enthusiastic. They try to maintain positive relations with the children and avoid directly controlling their behavior.

Yet commentary in Japan suggests that this model of preschooling is only one among several and that it may indeed by losing favor among certain segments of the population. Over the last twenty years, particularly, Japanese policymakers and educators have expressed concerns about the type of experiences children receive in preschool. Some deplore the group orientation of the "typical" preschool, arguing that Japanese children need to learn to be more creative and expressive if they are to flourish within the increasingly individualistic norms of modern society. Others criticize what they perceive to be the increasingly academic focus of some preschools, seeing their methods as a downward extension of the academic pressure that characterizes later grades. Their perception is that with little time to play and socialize with peers, preschoolers feel stressed and are not developing important social skills (Ishigaki, 1991, 1992). In response to these concerns about the lack of opportunity for creative expression and the downward extension of academic training, the Ministry of Education, which oversees preschools, issued guidelines in 1989 encouraging institutions to avoid academic training and to gear their programs to the individual needs, characteristics, and interests of each child.

The Western academic literature thus currently offers a portrait of preschools that does not match the perceptions within the Japanese educational community of important trends in early childhood education. The purpose of the project reported in this chapter was to explore the tension generated by these diverse views of appropriate practice. I wanted to find out more about the belief systems that guided the curriculum in Japanese preschools. Specifically, I sought to understand, from directors and teachers, what their goals and expectations were for the young children they were caring for. Also of interest was how they viewed the nature of the child and how they thought they could best stimulate learning and prepare a child for adult life in Japanese society. I wanted to determine how much variation there was among educators concerning these beliefs and how the beliefs were reflected in the curriculum and their relationships with children. This chapter reports on the findings pertaining to one type of preschool—schools that are guided by a philosophy that emphasizes the importance of fulfilling one's allotted societal role through sacrifice, hard work, and self-discipline. These role-centered schools, characterized by a heavy emphasis on academics and strict behavioral control, stand in stark contrast to the schools oriented toward developing children's social skills and those that focus primarily on nurturing personal growth and self-expression.

Capturing Variability Within Societies

Whereas some writers have been calling for studies of intracultural variation for years (for example, Pelto and Pelto, 1975), most researchers have lacked a theoretical framework for conceptualizing rule-governed heterogeneity below the level of the population and above the level of the individual. Recently, activity conducted under the rubric of cultural psychology provided a construal of culture as a medium offering a "rich input of heterogeneous social suggestions over the person's life course" (Valsiner and Litvinovic, 1996, p. 57). Formulations within a Vygotskian tradition bring theoretical sophistication to research on the diverse paths by which children learn to become adult members of a society, including culturally and historically derived tools as well as specific features of the current context and the active participation of societal members. Building on this interest in intracultural variation, those interested in the socialization of children in Japan have begun also to call for more careful examination of disagreements and differences within the society. Gjerde (1996) highlights variation within a society in communication scripts and developmental expectations of key socialization agents as well as in diverse features of activity settings. He argues that "national, cultural, and ethnic identity allow for considerable flexibility, interpersonal negotiation, and personal choice. . . . No complex culture is monolithic; each partakes of a measure of both concurrent variability and historical change and permits multiple activity settings that are not always well integrated" (p. 288).

The notion of *cultural models* is a helpful framework for characterizing the diversity of socialization beliefs and behaviors of adult members of a society. Cultural models are defined by Quinn and Holland (1987) as "presupposed, taken-for-granted models of the world that are widely shared (although not necessarily to the exclusion of other, alternative models) by members of a society and that play an enormous role in their understanding of that world and their behavior in it." Cultural models "frame experience, supplying interpretations of that experience and inferences about it, and [provide] goals for action" (p. 4). Cultural models are often associated with broad social categories like nation, gender, ethnicity, and social class. In addition, they can be specific to more narrowly bounded social contexts, for example, defined by neighborhood or workplace. Cultural models can also be conflicting and inconsistent, both within a society and within an individual (Kondo, 1990; Holloway, Fuller, Rambaud, and Eggers-Piérola, 1997). If we examine cultural models of early childhood education in Japan, the attributes of inconsistency, conflict, and ambiguity emerge just as they would in any society.

The individual plays an active role in appropriating cultural models from what Kojima (1986, 1988) has labeled the "ethnopsychological pool of ideas." This appropriation process is often considered to be tacit, as when a mother uses discipline strategies she experienced as a child without considering alternatives. However, child-rearing beliefs and practices often become the objects of conscious thought, becoming *declared models* as parents or other adults purposefully evaluate alternatives and adapt them to their current purposes (Holloway, Fuller, Rambaud, and Eggers-Piérola, 1997; see also Holloway and Minami, 1996). My project was designed to explore the varied models of education and socialization—both tacit and declared—that guide preschool directors and teachers.

Diverse Cultural Models

In the summer of 1994, I conducted interviews in thirty-two preschools and child-care centers in the Kansai region, which includes Osaka and Kobe. At each school, I interviewed the director and one or more teachers and conducted informal observations of four-year-olds in their classrooms. The interviews covered beliefs regarding individualization of teaching, the importance of academic preparation, techniques for discipline and control, and appropriate modes of teacher-child interaction. I selected four schools for a week each of more intensive observation—a child-care center, a public preschool, and two private preschools. The qualitative activity was followed up by obtaining a written questionnaire from roughly 150 preschool directors. This chapter focuses on the qualitative data.

Variation Across Preschools

I found many "typical" preschools that matched the description provided in earlier work—preschools in which warm teachers encouraged children to participate in group life through play and a small number of structured activities. But I also found two other distinct types, one that focused on identifying and developing the individual interests and abilities of each child and one that focused on teaching children the importance of fulfilling their societal roles, particularly the role of student.

The three types can be located along a dimension anchored by the two poles of *uchi* (inside) and *soto* (outside). To most Japanese people, *uchi* connotes a comfortable setting—most typically the home—where one can relax without worrying about what other people think. *Soto*, in contrast, connotes a public space in which the individual must restrain private impulses and faithfully execute the behaviors associated with a public role, such as employee, student, or parent (Quinn, 1994).

The preschools that many Japanese think of as "typical" contain a balance of both *uchi* and *soto* elements. I call them *society-centered* because they have the goal of preparing children for group life. As authors such as Peak (1991) have carefully described, teachers in these schools try to pull children gently out of the warm cocoon of family life and entice them with the rewards of being part of a larger group. Children in these schools spend each day playing freely outdoors and participating in one teacher-directed art activity (for example, gluing cotton balls to construction paper to create a snowy winter scene). The classroom usually contains desks or tables, a piano, and a small selection of manipulative toys. Art materials are not freely available; they are usually provided by the teacher only when it is time to engage in a specific activity. Much time and effort is spent helping children learn how to manage their possessions (for example, unpacking school bags, removing shoes before entering classroom), greet adults properly, use polite table manners, and participate in occasional group performances with their classmates. Teachers tend to talk to the group as a whole, or to subgroups, rather than initiate conversations with individual children.

A second type, the *child-centered* school, somewhat resembles Western play-oriented preschools. In response to societal changes and pressure from the Ministry of Education, directors of these schools have loosened up their programs and are moving to a more individualized approach. Directors report that they are attempting to create a feeling of warmth, dependence on adults (*amae*), and informality that typically characterizes mother-child relations in Japan (Doi, 1973). These schools are usually public and are often run by women who were formerly teachers. Children in these schools spend much of the day engaged in free play. Unlike society-centered preschools, where children's art activities are conducted in a large-group format, the child-centered schools tend to be set up in activity corners for individual children or a small number of children. The classrooms contain manipulatives, a variety of art materials, and supplies for fantasy play. There are few group activities—performances are kept to a minimum and group time before dismissal may often be spent with individual children recounting what they had made or done that day. Communication between the teacher and individual children is frequent.

This chapter will focus primarily on a third type—those on the *soto* end of the dimension. This type, the *role-centered* preschool, has not been described in previous literature. Yet it represents a crucial element of the early socialization process in Japan. A preschool director active in a regional private preschool association estimated that perhaps 30 percent of private preschools are role-centered. Unlike their colleagues in child-centered schools, directors of role-centered preschools eschew individualism and other Western ideas of appropriate practice. The philosophy that guides the Japanese role-oriented preschool directors can be traced back to ideologies that have been salient in Japan for many years.

In role-centered preschools, staff members teach children to fulfill the requirements of the role they are supposed to occupy in a given situation. Because the role of student is a very important one for Japanese children, much of the time in these preschools is devoted to preparing children for elementary school. The six role-centered schools I visited were all private, and three were run by Buddhist monks. In five of the six, the directors were men. Three of the directors expressed conservative political beliefs. These schools were popular in Kansai; four of the six had more than five hundred students. The curriculum was more oriented toward academic preparation than in the other two types of schools. In addition to studying reading, writing, and mathematics, children were given a choice of lessons in such areas as English, art, tea ceremony, gymnastics, swordsmanship, and traditional Japanese dance. The directors of these schools were openly critical if not contemptuous of the Ministry of Education and claimed to be purposely ignorant of—or in disagreement with—ministry guidelines.

Portrait of a Role-Centered Preschool

The philosophy and activities of role-oriented preschools can best be conveyed by presenting a detailed portrait of a particular school. (Please note that names and certain distinguishing features have been changed to preserve the anonymity of the schools and staff members.) Wakaba Preschool is one of the schools I selected for a week of intense observation. It is located an hour's train ride from downtown Kobe. The main buildings form an L shape around two sides of the large playground. A third side is bordered by a new wing for the five-year-olds. A well-tended garden edges the fourth side. The playground is mostly open space, with a large wooden climbing structure, a sand area, and a few small structures for pretend play. Numerous large windows in each building let air and light into the corridors that run along the front of both floors. The school contains eleven classrooms—two for three-year-olds, four for four-year-olds, and five for five-year-olds. Class sizes range from twenty-eight in the three-year-old classes to forty in the five-year-old classes.

Models of Self and Other in Role-Centered Preschools

The director of Wakaba Preschool, Mr. Waseda, explained the philosophy guiding his preschool in a series of interviews during the week of observation. His central conviction was that Japanese children must be brought up to perform whatever role they are allocated in life with diligence, confidence, and competence. He drew on the image of the traditional Japanese artisan (*shokunin*)—the gardener, carpenter, or sushi chef—arguing that the children at his preschool should become like the artisan whose work-defined role provides a guide for how to live and a source of motivation to try one's hardest. Mr. Waseda explained how the notion of role identification could lead to a strong society by creating a unified populace, each of whom contributes unique qualities to the betterment of the group:

> We need to create a feeling of harmony [*wa*] among people but not simply conformity [*dou*]. With *wa* we can communicate, but our individual identity remains clear. With *dou* we overlap and blend together too much. Agreement exists with doubts. To get *wa* we need to have a clear understanding and acceptance of our role. If one person is clear who he is he can join with another to create something new. If he is wishy-washy about who he is he can't synchronize with anyone. . . . We need to revive the idea held by traditional artisans, who have a strong feeling of responsibility toward their trade and pride in their skills. . . . It is good to have the artisanal spirit [*shokunin katagi*]. We need the strength to find and go our own way.

Mr. Waseda emphasized that one must learn to perform one's role, even when one operates "in the shadows," that is, if one's efforts are behind the scenes rather than in the bright light where they are more easily recognized and appreciated. At the same time, it is essential for everyone to develop a "mind of appreciation" toward those who quietly perform their duties.

> One phrase we repeat often here concerns the importance of helping others, without saying anything. In doing so, our own mind becomes brighter. By doing this, children will feel thanks to their parents and will do things for others. This gets below the surface and helps them learn the deep lesson of helping others. Some people work very hard behind the scenes, like trash collectors, for example. They are "in the shade" and may not be seen. People like this are very important. There is a Buddhist saying, "We bless from the bottom of our feet." It refers to the fact that the undersides of your feet—which are in the shade and cannot be seen—are crucial because we cannot stand without being strong there. These days, people only want to look at the bright things that are in the light. We need to have feelings for things that are below the surface. And do things without being seen by others. Don't be conscious only of the parts you can see.

Within the *shokunin* idiom, the spotlight is on the artisan's whole-hearted fulfillment of the role requirements without an expectation of individual recognition. This orientation is not compatible with the expression of individual, divergent views. The directors of role-oriented schools tended to think that Western-style individualism is inappropriate for Japan. As one director said,

"After World War Two, the Japanese people made the mistake of seeking only freedom. We misunderstood that there is a strict aspect of freedom. Freedom is not easy."

Mr. Waseda expressed similar sentiments. He regretted that Japanese people had lost their ability to behave in a role-directed manner (*Nihonjin-rashisa*) in the years following the war. For him, knowledge of one's role led one not only to know how to behave but also to know how one felt. To his teachers, he emphasized the importance of embracing the role requirements at the deepest level of feeling: "She [a teacher] must know her own feelings. If she has the feeling of being quiet, it will come through to the children. The feeling behind the words is important."

Learning to fulfill one's role does not connote weakness or passive acceptance of the rules dictated by society. To the role-oriented directors, only by actively committing oneself to one's role-dictated responsibilities can the individual become strong. These men believed that the materialism, permissiveness, and individualism of each successive generation have led to the weakening of the Japanese people and to the weakness of Japan as a world power. The director at Wakaba spoke passionately of his desire to recover the Japanese strength of the past, a strength rooted in a uniquely Japanese secular ideology: "I want to reestablish the real Japanese culture. We need to find the one straight path [*ikkansei*] for the Japanese. If you are in a culture with a strong religion you can establish a strong philosophy of life. But the Japanese don't have a strong religion. Japan needs to find its *ikkansei* in order to be respected. We should stop being wishy-washy like Japanese politicians these days. We need a strong pole."

Theories of Pedagogy

One element common to all role-centered schools is the notion that children should be exposed to many experiences rather than participate primarily in activities that they already like. Directors in the society- and child-centered schools tended to talk about the importance of building on children's strengths. In the role-centered schools, directors were more concerned with strengthening the children's weak points, a view put forth by the director of a large role-oriented preschool in Osaka:

> Many people criticize me because I lack a focus on individuality. If a child likes drawing pictures then it is his or her choice to do that. But drawing pictures and doing nothing else is utterly wrong. Children should establish solid basics, then each individual's particular characteristics will grow. Energy and persistence should be nurtured. . . . Our motto is that they should come to like everything. I certainly believe that strengthening the areas children [already] like is education. But I believe that helping children overcome dislikes is education in the real sense. . . . A group helps individuals overcome their dislikes.

This director drew a connection between strengthening a child's weak points and situating instruction in the context of a group. He rejected the type of individualized instruction endorsed by child-centered directors, believing that children who are given individual treatment will simply persist in the behaviors and way of thinking they prefer rather than broaden their interests. He made a strong argument in favor of group-oriented education: "Our basic principle is group education. The teacher does not raise individual children. Instead children learn from the group. Therefore it is essential to create a good group and from the good group good individuals grow."

Creating Conditions of Challenge or Hardship

One of the stated principles underlying the Ministry of Education guidelines is that the school environment should be warm and supportive in order to allow a child to express himself or herself confidently. This principle was endorsed by the child-centered schools. As the director of one child-centered preschool told me, the main goal of her school was setting up an environment for children to play in a carefree (*nobi-nobi*) manner while they had the chance. The role-centered preschools did not appear to be guided by this principle. They subscribed to the traditional Japanese notion that experiencing hardship (*kurou*) was an essential part of moving from the self-centeredness of childhood to the social responsibility of adulthood. The children at Wakaba were expected to sit for long periods of time and to perform activities dictated by the teacher rather than by personal choice. They were challenged to train for marathons, run obstacle courses, or perform other demanding tasks. Similar physical challenges were purposely created in a large role-centered preschool in Osaka, where the annual three-day field trip took the children "into a wilderness that is full of danger . . . where they ford a river and climb a steep mountain." The director explained why experiences of hardship were needed in preschool, and explicitly distinguished his point of view from that of the *uchi*-oriented preschools:

> Today's affluent and free society robs children of their independence. Adults intervene in children's activities and try to protect them too much. . . . Early childhood education in Japan tends to analyze children from the adult's viewpoint; they analyze them and try to protect them. . . . They spoil children's inherent energy. . . . [In the past] children used to grow without as much parental care. The environment was suitable for children's growth, in terms of nature as well as society and home. For example, hard domestic labor was a good environment for children. Hard circumstances such as many siblings, poverty, and less parental attention caused severe competition among siblings. Although there was less parental care there was an abundant amount of nature. Nowadays because of Westernization we have fewer children and nuclear families. Mothers do not have to do anything. Everything is instant. Japanese children will be bad, or they have already become bad. Therefore correcting that predicament is our goal.

Models of Control

In child- and society-centered preschools, teachers tend to avoid expressing their authority in overt ways. They are likely to ignore misbehavior or to rely on peers to sanction a classmate. In cases of serious transgressions they may try reasoning or gentle but persistent persuasion; their goal is not to achieve behavioral compliance but to help the child understand the benefits of good behavior. Peak has likened teachers in these schools to "an army of friendly shadows" who appear to yield to the child's desire but eventually win by prolonged, good-natured cajoling (Peak, 1991). Peak describes how the teachers she observed shied away from labeling children as "problems" and avoided isolating or chastising them. These tactics are echoed in studies of Japanese mothers, whose permissiveness relative to Western mothers has frequently been noted (Smith and Wiswell, 1982; Conroy, Hess, Azuma, and Kashiwagi, 1980).

The teachers at Wakaba employed these same strategies much of the time. They were expected to be cheerful, smiling, and energetic. They generally tried to encourage the children to participate by presenting material in a very organized manner, maintaining a snappy pace, and persistently encouraging children who were slow or unwilling to go along with the program. However, the role-centered schools required children to move through the daily program in the specified manner. This led the teachers in those schools to resort at times to more authoritarian tactics; in particular, they tended to issue threats, which they rarely carried out.

The relatively permissive orientation of the teachers contrasted with the authoritarian behavior of the administrative staff. The members of the administration and the teachers of special subjects at Wakaba used physical punishment, praise and criticism, labeling, and surveillance, illustrated in the following excerpt from an observation of a singing lesson:

> The music specialist, Mr. Yamagi, comes once a month to instruct the children and teachers in choral singing. Barely five feet tall and seventy-five years old, he cuts a dramatic figure with long wavy hair, a large turquoise ring, and a flowing silk kerchief. Mr. Yamagi catches sight of me when I enter the rear of this class of four-year-olds and announces in full hearing of the students that this room contains four "problem children," whom he then points out. He indicates their names on a school memorandum listing students "in need of observation" *(you kansatsu ji)*. He runs over to one of the four and pulls him in front of me, saying, "He doesn't have any energy, so it's hard work to give him energy. It's important to educate him." He turns to the boy for confirmation, "Right?" The boy shifts uneasily and mumbles. Mr. Yamagi pulls the boy to the front of the class and grabs his hand, uncurling the fingers and raising it straight into the air. "Say 'Yes!' like this," Mr. Yamagi yells enthusiastically, still holding the boy's hand up in the air. "Yes!" says the boy in a high-pitched voice. "You see," says Mr. Yamagi, looking at me, "we have to train them how to answer."

When the lesson is over, Mr. Yamagi rushes to another class of four-year-olds. They are sitting cross-legged on the floor, silently awaiting his arrival. As he crosses the threshold, the classroom teacher strikes a chord on the piano, an indication to the children that they should bow. Mr. Yamagi bows crisply, then strides over to a child whose bowing has displeased him, saying, "If you don't bow correctly you may leave." He asks him to bow again, then smacks him lightly on the cheek. He turns briefly to the observers and adds an aside: "A good class of children doesn't say anything."

Mr. Yamagi used many tactics for preventing misbehavior, including careful surveillance, humiliation, criticism, and physical sanctions. Surveillance was also a key activity for the director, Mr. Waseda. A stern man, he invariably dressed formally, in a dark navy suit and tie. He rarely spoke to any children during my observation periods other than to sanction them for misbehavior. He spent a great deal of time observing teachers and students, making corrections when behavior did not meet his expectations. For example, during the morning meeting in the school yard, he would pull children back into line if they started to straggle, or tap them on the shoulder to indicate a need for straighter posture. When the children returned to classes, the dark figure of Mr. Waseda could be seen passing by the windows along one side of the classroom, glancing into each. At music rehearsals, the classroom teachers crouched down unobtrusively and shuttled up and down the lines of singing children, correcting posture, straightening the lines, and silently mouthing the words to the song while smiling in an exaggerated manner. Mr. Waseda also patrolled the rows, shaking a finger at the child who was talking, and occasionally removing a particularly rowdy child from the room for a scolding. At Wakaba, the relatively permissive styles of the teachers and the strict administrators combined to create a system of control familiar to Americans as a "good cop—bad cop" routine.

Tension, Conflict, and Resistance in Role-Oriented Preschools

The core philosophy driving the program at Wakaba reflected one side of a dynamic tension within Japanese society regarding the essential definition of what it means to be Japanese. Mr. Waseda constructed a vision of his school by drawing on images from the distant Japanese past. He saw himself as strenuously resisting Western influences responsible for the declining character of the Japanese people. He also believed that there were serious flaws in the Japanese way of thinking that made them particularly vulnerable to negative elements of Western democracy. One of his primary opponents was the Ministry of Education, particularly because of their efforts to get schools to individualize instruction, nurture creativity and personal expression, and develop an international mentality.

Mr. Waseda also found himself in conflict with many of the mothers whose children attended his school. Some observers have maintained that

Japanese mothers and preschool staff have worked out a harmonious complementary relationship. Mothers are said to foster close relations with children through maintaining physical proximity and avoiding confrontation; they do not try to initiate or prepare children for life in the group. Teachers, it is said, do not try to replicate the mother's close relationship; rather, they act as midwives to assist the child's entry into the group (Peak, 1991; Tobin, Wu, and Davidson, 1989). This image of smooth integration was not expressed by the school directors I interviewed, who felt strongly that mothers were overly permissive and either neglectful or overly protective of their children. Most of the directors—from all types of preschools—held very negative views about modern parents and were pessimistic about the fate of the Japanese family. The directors frequently held in contempt mothers who were either too spoiled and self-centered or too insecure to raise their children properly. They did not perceive any possibility of a meaningful partnership, nor did they see their roles as complementary with those of mothers. Rather, they were so convinced of mothers' inadequacy that they felt the only realistic solution was to bypass them completely and attempt to influence the children as profoundly as possible through the daily school program. The following quotation from the head teacher in a role-oriented Buddhist preschool is typical:

> Mothers are young and have a lot of information about early childhood education. They want to educate their children in the way they believe works best, but this way may not fit well with Japanese classrooms. Since they each have a particular view, there is no clear consensus, and they make a variety of requests. They are very enthusiastic about after-school programs and lessons like violin and tea ceremony. However, they tend to ignore the importance of discipline. They seem to assume that preschool teachers discipline their children. They want to enjoy their own lives, and they have jobs. They think they can buy discipline.

The relations between the director and the teachers also contained an element of tension, although one that was considerably more hidden. Following the usual preschool practice, the director at Wakaba avoided teachers who had worked in other preschools; he preferred to draw new teachers from the pool of young women who had just received an associate's degree in early childhood education in order to obtain full allegiance to the ideas and practices developed by the director for his particular school. The teachers at Wakaba appeared compliant and typically did not initiate any criticism of the school or the director. Only one teacher openly stated to us her concerns about the program: "Children here don't have any time to play or to be with their teacher. They are never encouraged to think. And the teachers get in trouble if they ever let the children talk or do what they want." Referring to an incident in which she threatened to leave the classroom if the children didn't stop talking, she said, "I don't like to tell the children I'm going to leave them like that."

A third level of tension and resistance can be noted by watching the children. In contrast to the boisterous activity that characterized the child- and society-oriented preschools, schools like Wakaba were usually quiet and orderly. However, there were occasional eruptions of misbehavior, and in the Rabbit class, one child, Kohei, was frequently in the thick of these. He had a ready smile but also a slight swagger to his step, and he gave the impression of an intense enjoyment of life. Kohei used humor and daring to entrance the other children and often succeeded in charming the teacher even as he was doing something mischievous. One of Kohei's primary roles in the classroom was to mediate disputes among the children. The following excerpt illustrates how Kohei managed the underground world of peer relations, where small dramas were enacted as a subtext beneath the official world of learning.

> Ms. Watanabe is explaining an art project to the class. Each child will receive a paper with an oval shape drawn on it. They will be asked to fill in the facial features of their own fathers. She passes out paper, and the children begin to draw. After ten minutes, one girl, Miki, starts crying and leans over to cover her paper, hiding it from view of her classmates. The others at her table look concerned, and I hear them whisper, "Get Kohei." Someone brings over Kohei and explains that Noboru has made fun of Miki's drawing. Kohei listens, nods, and slugs Noboru on the arm, then turns to pat Miki briefly on the head. He turns and strides back to his table. The teacher is busy with children on the other side of the room and apparently hasn't noticed any of this.

Kohei's behavior helps us remember that even in tightly controlled classrooms, children find small spaces of resistance. The teachers and staff at Wakaba monitored and regulated children's group behavior and also gave somewhat ritualized control to children in the form of the daily monitors (*touban*). However, the children themselves created an alternative, hidden layer of control that enabled them to manage interpersonal disputes without needing to rely on adults.

The various levels of tension and conflict at Wakaba illustrate how resistance to authority can occur simultaneously with submission to authority, even in environments where cultural models for behavior are clearly articulated and enforced. Western writers have tended to classify individuals as *either* accepting norms mandated by authority *or* rejecting those norms, or they have tended to develop neat categories of action, such as resistance, coping, and consent. Kondo (1990) argues that in complex social settings, "people consent, cope and resist at different levels of consciousness at a single point in time" (p. 224). Japanese individuals are sometimes portrayed as outwardly submitting to authority while inwardly resisting authority. A more likely scenario is that their resistance is fragmented and situationally differentiated and that it is often combined—within the same person—with endorsement and incorporation of dominant norms and practices.

Conclusions

The need to strike a balance between the rights, desires, and needs of the individual and the smooth functioning of the group has been a persistent theme throughout Japan's history—as it is throughout all human societies. These data reveal the struggle of thirty-two individual directors to come to their own understanding of this balance, and illustrate the process by which they incorporate "traditional" Japanese values and practices into their programs. The data also reflect the diverse results of this process.

The beliefs and practices of the role-oriented directors are an important part of the story of socialization in Japan. The authoritarian techniques used by the staff at Wakaba to control the children's behavior are found in many other Japanese settings as well, including cram schools and professional and amateur athletics. These settings also feature experiences of hardship (*kurou*), exhortation combined with strict punishment, and high expectations for achievement (Rohlen, 1983, p. 192; Smith, 1994). A close look at the literature suggests that corporal punishment and surveillance are also widespread in middle and high schools (Mouer and Sugimoto, 1986), in spite of being outlawed after World War Two. Feiler (1991) describes one survey in which three-quarters of Japanese teachers admitted using corporal punishment (p. 246), in spite of the fact that it has been outlawed for half a century.

The dual strands of indulgence and authoritarianism are conveyed in a Japanese proverb advocating the use of *ame to muchi*, or "candy and the whip." The relative strength of each of these two elements in any particular socialization setting depends on the historical period and the region, as well as on characteristics of the caregivers and context. In any given setting, there may be a degree of acceptance of the balance, but there will also be dissent, renegotiation, and change. The key point is not to gloss over the vigor and importance of this debate. By paying attention to the wide range of voices, and listening—not just for harmony but also for diversity, disagreement, and even resistance—we can learn many new things about Japan.

References

Boocock, S. S. "Controlled Diversity: An Overview of the Japanese Preschool System." *Journal of Japanese Studies*, 1989, *15*, 41–65.

Conroy, M., Hess, R. D., Azuma, H., and Kashiwagi, K. "Maternal Strategies for Regulating Children's Behavior: Japanese and American Families." *Journal of Cross-Cultural Psychology*, 1980, *11*, 153–172.

Doi, T. *The Anatomy of Dependence*. Tokyo: Kodansha International, 1973.

Feiler, B. S. *Learning to Bow: Inside the Heart of Japan*. New York: Ticknor & Fields, 1991.

Gjerde, P. F. "Longitudinal Research in a Cultural Context: Reflections, Prospects, Challenges." In D. Shwalb and B. Shwalb (eds.), *Japanese Childrearing: Two Generations of Scholarship*. New York: Guilford Press, 1996.

Hendry, J. *Becoming Japanese: The World of the Preschool Child*. Honolulu: University of Hawaii Press, 1986.

Holloway, S. D., Fuller, B., Rambaud, M. F., and Eggers-Pérola, C. *Through My Own Eyes: Single Mothers and the Cultures of Poverty*. Cambridge, Mass.: Harvard University Press, 1997.

Holloway, S. D., and Minami, M. "Production and Reproduction of Culture: The Dynamic Role of Mothers and Children in Early Socialization." In D. Shwalb and B. Shwalb (eds.), *Japanese Childrearing: Two Generations of Scholarship*. New York: Guilford Press, 1996.

Ishigaki, E. H. "The Historical Stream of Early Childhood Pedagogic Concepts in Japan." *Early Child Development and Care*, 1991, 75, 121–159.

Ishigaki, E. H. "The Preparation of Early Childhood Teachers in Japan. Part 1: What Is the Goal of Early Childhood Care and Education in Japan?" *Early Child Development and Care*, 1992, 78, 111–138.

Kojima, H. "Japanese Concepts of Child Development from the Mid-17th to Mid-19th Century." *International Journal of Behavioral Development*, 1986, 9, 315–329.

Kojima, H. "The Role of Belief-Value Systems Related to Child-Rearing and Education: The Case of Early Modern to Modern Japan." In D. Sinha and H.S.R. Kao (eds.), *Social Values and Development: Asian Perspectives*. Thousand Oaks, Calif.: Sage, 1988.

Kondo, D. K. *Crafting Selves: Power, Gender, and Discourses of Identity in a Japanese Workplace*. Chicago: University of Chicago Press, 1990.

Lewis, C. C. *Educating Hearts and Minds: Reflections on Japanese Preschool and Elementary Education*. Cambridge, Mass.: Cambridge University Press, 1995.

Markus, H. R., and Kitayama, S. "Culture and the Self: Implications for Cognition, Emotion, and Motivation." *Psychological Review*, 1991, 98, 224–253.

Mouer, R., and Sugimoto, Y. *Images of Japanese Society: A Study in the Social Construction of Reality*. London: Kegan Paul, 1986.

Peak, L. *Learning to Go to School in Japan: The Transition from Home to Preschool Life*. Berkeley: University of California Press, 1991.

Pelto, P. J., and Pelto, G. H. "Intra-Cultural Diversity: Some Theoretical Issues." *American Ethnologist*, 1975, 2, 1–18.

Quinn, C. J., Jr. "The Terms *Uchi* and *Soto* as Windows on a World." In J. M. Bachnik and C. J. Quinn Jr. (eds.), *Situated Meaning: Inside and Outside in Japanese Self, Society, and Language*. Princeton, N.J.: Princeton University Press, 1994.

Quinn, N., and Holland, D. "Culture and Cognition." In D. Holland and N. Quinn (eds.), *Cultural Models in Language and Thought*. Cambridge, Mass.: Cambridge University Press, 1987.

Rohlen, T. P. *Japan's High Schools*. Berkeley: University of California Press, 1983.

Smith, H. W. *The Myth of Japanese Homogeneity: Social-Ecological Diversity in Education and Socialization*. Commack, N.Y.: Nova Science, 1994.

Smith, R. J., and Wiswell, E. L. *The Women of Suye Mura*. Chicago: University of Chicago Press, 1982.

Stevenson, H. W., and Stigler, J. *The Learning Gap: Why Our Schools Are Failing and What We Can Learn from Japanese and Chinese Education*. New York: Summit, 1992.

Tobin, J. J., Wu, D.Y.H., and Davidson, D. H. *Preschool in Three Cultures: Japan, China, and the United States*. New Haven, Conn.: Yale University Press, 1989.

Valsiner, J., and Litvinovic, G. "Processes of Generalization in Parental Reasoning." In S. Harkness and C. M. Super (eds.), *Parents' Cultural Belief Systems: Their Origins, Expressions, and Consequences*. New York: Guilford Press, 1996.

SUSAN D. HOLLOWAY is adjunct professor of education at the University of California, Berkeley.

Cultures include a combination of shared and contested understandings. Although individuals may identify with their culture, they are also critical of practices judged unfair. Cultural practices that privilege one group and restrict the practices of another are sources of conflict and change.

Conflict, Social Development, and Cultural Change

Elliot Turiel

It is generally assumed that morality pertains to evaluations and judgments about right and wrong or good and bad. Within the context of this general assumption, there are many differences in philosophical and social scientific propositions regarding the nature of moral evaluations and judgments. Among psychologists, especially, there are differences in propositions regarding sources of the acquisition of morality. Accordingly, the development of morality has been a critical issue in theoretical formulations and research for psychologists (Freud, 1930; Piaget, 1932; Skinner, 1971). Given that morality pertains to relationships among people and that it is a collective enterprise, moral development has been closely linked to formulations of culture and differences between cultures. However, because morality is often regarded as pertaining to how people should act, rather than how they do act, explanations of moral development can pose challenges to conceptions of culture.

The reason morality, insofar as it bears on "oughts" (how people should act) and not only on what exists (how people do act), can pose such a challenge is that culture is often construed to be based on what exists—on agreed-on standards and common ways of acting. Culture is said to entail *shared* understandings among members of a group that provide solidarity, cohesion, and harmony. As an example, it has been maintained that there is agreement "that culture consists of *shared* elements that provide the standards for perceiving, believing, evaluating, communicating, and acting among those who share a language, historic period, and geographic location" (Triandis, 1996, p. 408). The shared elements include social practices that are part of the moral codes or standards of cultures. Frequently, several differences in accepted standards among cultures are cited to illustrate the cultural sources of moral codes.

Among these are polygamy, arranged marriages, divorce, widow remarriage, wearing of the veil, female virginity, and contact between people of different castes. It is said that different cultures have taken very different positions on the morality of these types of actions. In some cultures there is abhorrence of a given act, whereas in others there is acceptance.

In pointing to these types of social practices as ones that often represent differences between cultures, it is explicitly (sometimes implicitly) assumed that there is general agreement about them within a culture. It is important to note, however, that many of these practices serve to restrict the activities and autonomy of a group of persons (for example, women, persons of lower caste) and that they bear on the nature of relationships between groups of persons (for example, females and males, persons of lower caste and upper caste). Moreover, it is not at all clear that there are shared understandings regarding many of these types of practices or that there is harmony around them. Do women and men, for example, make the same evaluations about practices like polygamy, arranged marriages, divorce, and many of the other restrictions applied to females? With regard to gender issues, Okin (1989, p. 67) asserts that in contemporary society in the United States there are "no shared understandings." In Okin's view, hierarchical arrangements between males and females, as well as other social arrangements of power, status, and influence, make for differences in perspectives within cultures: "Oppressor and oppressed—when the voices of the latter can be heard at all—often disagree fundamentally" (p. 67). Along with gender, socioeconomic differences are likely to make for "contested" understandings and conflicts. Furthermore, in many cultures, social hierarchy involves a complex interaction of gender and social class, affecting relationships in the workplace and economic status (Chen, 1995).

Differences in perspectives among people can stem from differences in positions of power, influence, and status in the social hierarchy. In turn, such differences can result in deep tensions that lead to cultural change. In this chapter, I focus on "contested" understandings, conflicts, and disharmony, which I propose are as central to cultural participation as shared understandings and harmonious relationships. Such contested meanings and social conflicts often have a basis in moral judgments and can result in cultural transformations. One of the significant sources of change in cultural practices is the conflicts and tensions engendered by the nature of those very practices.

Cultural Comparisons and Coherence

Whether we can even speak of changes in cultures has been quite controversial. In part, it has been controversial because it is difficult to assess when change has occurred and to explain how it might occur. It has also proven difficult to assess whether changes, assuming they occur, can be termed *development* or *progressive*. Edelstein, in Chapter One of this volume, discusses some criteria for progressive societal changes through historical epochs. He also shows that changes can be of a regressive kind. Both Saxe and Greenfield (Chapters Two and Three) consider relations between individual cognitive development and changes in cultural practices. In concluding her essay, Greenfield draws an interesting distinction between cultural changes that are directional and those that might constitute progress in the human condition. By directional change, she means that societies in the world are tending to change in particular ways (such as toward greater commercialization). Progress implies some improvement in the human condition.

For many years, however, analyses of culture gave little consideration to directional or progressive changes. In large measure, this is because of some of the ways cultural change, progress, and differences were portrayed in the latter part of the nineteenth century and early part of the twentieth century. At that time, there was a tendency for Westerners to order cultures on an evolutionary scale, placing Western cultures at the most advanced levels with regard to both intellectual and moral functioning. During the first part of the twentieth century, several cultural anthropologists became highly critical of such orderings on the grounds that no criteria existed for considering Western cultures as superior. It was argued that the orderings reflected a bias for one's own point of view, such that one's own values were the standard of comparison and were placed at the highest end without recognition that other cultures' values are different and equally valid.

Two perhaps contradictory sets of ideas were invoked through these critiques. One idea was that cultures form coherent integrated patterns, which serve to distinguish them from each other. As put by Benedict (1934, p. 36): "The significance of cultural behavior is not exhausted when we have clearly understood that it is local and manmade and highly variable. It tends also to be integrated. A culture, like an individual, is a more or less consistent pattern of thought and action." The proposition of consistent or integrated patterns implied cultural and moral relativism—that there are no standards by which the values of different cultures can be compared.

A second set of ideas invoked in these analyses, along with the accusations of bias in favor of one's own culture in hierarchical orderings, was moral and nonrelativistic—namely, that the orderings reflected intolerance, a lack of respect for other cultures, and failure to appreciate equal worth. As several commentators have pointed out (Hatch, 1983; Schmidt, 1955), positions of cultural relativism often involve moral prescriptions. In particular, underlying the position is the assertion of the values of tolerance (that the validity of other cultures' values and perspectives should be accepted), freedom (that a culture should not be obstructed from following its moral standards), and equality (that a cultures' moral standards should be regarded as of equal validity to any other). These principles are evident in the following statement (Herskovitz, 1947, as quoted in Hatch, 1983, p. 86): "Cultural relativism is a philosophy which, in recognizing the values set up by every society to guide its own life, lays stress on the dignity inherent in every body of custom, and on the need for tolerance of conventions though they may differ from one's own. . . . The relativistic point of view brings into relief the validity of every set of norms for the people whose lives are guided by them, and the values they represent."

These propositions of cultural anthropologists highlighted the inadequacies of hierarchical orderings of cultures and the possibility that the values of Westerners were simply assumed to be more advanced (without providing criteria for the comparisons). In the effort to argue that cultures differed in ways that could not be compared on an evolutionary scale, it was also proposed that cultures constitute cohesive, integrated, and largely harmonious ways of thinking and acting. The idea of coherence has had a long-term influence on portrayals of cultures, which persists in contemporary analyses of cultural differences in moral and personal understandings (Kitayama and Markus, 1994; Markus and Kitayama, 1991; Shweder and Haidt, 1993; Triandis, 1990, 1996). It is also an idea that has come under scrutiny and criticism. Disagreements among social scientists (especially among anthropologists) have been voiced as to whether cultures are adequately characterized as entailing shared understandings, cohesiveness, and harmony (Abu-Lughod, 1991; Appadurai, 1988; Spiro, 1993; Strauss, 1992; Wikan, 1991). As Wikan (1991, p. 289) put it: "Order reigned, at the expense of uncertainties, ambiguities, contesting visions, not to speak of the disorder and unpredictability of much of everyday life. Norms, rules, and regularities carried the day to coalesce into a harmonious whole of pattern, consistency—in short, a culture. . . . Eyes set on cosmic balance, it is not easy to keep track of messy, murky, mundane realities, as I can vouch for myself. The same goes when other elevated concepts like 'honor,' or 'hierarchy,' or today's guest of honor—'culture'—are in focus."

Wikan believes that a shift in approach is necessary. It is a shift that would be difficult because "it entails modifying die-hard habits of work and moving down the social ladder away from association with 'culture's' spokesmen and evocateurs to more ordinary people of humdrum, inostensible concerns" (p. 290). A theme of much import is emerging, which is consonant with Okin's assertions (1989) that especially among oppressors and oppressed there are many disagreements about fundamental issues and that insufficient attention is given to the perspectives of those in positions of lesser power and influence in the social hierarchy: "And so it is that the concept of culture as a seamless whole and of society as a bounded group manifesting inherently valued order and normatively regulated response, effectively masked human misery and quenched dissenting voices" (Wikan, 1991, p. 290).

The moral imperatives asserted by cultural relativists—that cultures should be accorded tolerance, freedom, and equality—become relevant here. It has been noted that these moral imperatives constitute an internal contradiction of the relativistic position. Perhaps more important, if it is the case that within cultures not all is uniform, that greater rights and privileges are accorded to some groups than others, and that there are different perspectives, then it would follow that, at a minimum, the moral considerations said to apply to different cultural groups would also apply to different groups within cultures. Different groups of people, defined by social structural categories in the social hierarchy (for example, females and males, lower classes or castes and higher classes or castes) may represent different interests and goals. Insofar as conflicts and contested understandings exist, the issues of tolerance, freedom, and equality may be applicable.

Dissent and Seams

Are the voices of people in positions lacking power, influence, and status dissenting ones, and does this render culture not a seamless whole? For cultures to be seamless—that is, to be coherent and harmonious—it would mean that individuals' social development is largely a consequence of participation in the culture. Individuals would thus acquire a general orientation shared among them. We do know that in most of the world's cultures there are differences in social positions and that distinctions, with inequalities, exist among groups of people. As already noted, social hierarchical differences exist between males and females and people of different socioeconomic classes. However, the fact of social differences does not, in itself, mean that cultures are not coherent or harmonious. It may be that people in different positions in a social hierarchy accept things as they are and have a common perspective on cultural practices and the varying privileges and burdens. As an example, Shweder, Mahapatra, and Miller (1987) took the position that both males and females in a traditional culture (such as in India) accept the hierarchy in the family, much as they would accept hierarchy in a military unit. Therefore, it is said that they accept cultural practices permitting a husband to beat his wife "black and blue" for engaging in disobedient acts. Extending this line of argument more generally, Shweder, Much, Mahapatra, and Park (1997) maintained that acceptance of social hierarchy is based on appreciation of the benefits of asymmetrical reciprocity. The social hierarchy is accepted by all because those in dominant positions are obligated to promote and protect the welfare of those in subordinate positions, while, in turn, those in subordinate positions are obligated to serve those in dominant positions; for example, "Wives should be obedient to their husbands, and husbands should be sensitive and responsive to the needs, desires, and inclinations of their wives" (Shweder, Much, Mahapatra, and Park, 1997, p. 145).

All this would make sense if it were the case that growing up in a culture, people mainly acquire the public and dominant view of how to be and how to act morally. The idea that those in subordinate positions accept as their own the strict rules of obedience and asymmetrical reciprocity rests on the assumption that cultures largely shape concepts of persons (including the self) and moral judgments. That is, people in different cultures form different conceptions of persons, self, and morality. The major differences proposed have been between independent and interdependent concepts of persons and between moralities based on rights and on duties. In contrast with modern Western cultures, where independence, autonomy, and individuality are emphasized, in traditional cultures persons are subsumed within the social order in a system of interdependent relationships. It is a cultural framework of interdependence, with persons connected to shared goals, that makes for a willing, unconflicted, and uncontested acceptance of subordination. Morality in such traditional cultures is based mainly on fulfilling specified duties and maintaining the social order. Hence inequalities and the burdens that may come with holding positions of subordination (for example, based on gender or social class) are not approached from the viewpoints of moral concerns with equality, fairness, or rights.

However, if people in traditional cultures do form concepts of persons and self that include concerns with independence, autonomy, and the attainment of personal goals, and if they do develop judgments about fairness and rights, then conflicts and contested understandings may exist within those cultures. It would suggest, as Okin, Wikan, and others have said, that culture is not seamless, cohesive, or without dissent. It is a consequence of researchers' tendencies to look to public symbols or ideologies and to the perspectives of those in dominance that the diversity of concepts of persons and morality has been overlooked. It is also a consequence of a failure to recognize that everyone does not participate in the "culture" in the same ways.

Consider concepts of persons and self with regard to public pronouncements or ideologies. The general claim (for example, Geertz, 1984) has been that a distinction needs to be drawn between cultures with concepts of persons as bounded (clear distinctiveness of persons and an emphasis on separateness) and those in which persons are seen as unbounded (no contrasts of self from others). However, it has also been noted by Spiro (1993) that much of the evidence in support of this distinction comes from research that has focused on conceptions of self through analyses of cultural symbols or ideologies. Spiro maintains further that there is some research in non-Western cultures demonstrating that individuals do hold conceptions of persons as independent and autonomous (bounded). An example of how individuals' experiences and conceptions do not necessarily correspond to cultural conceptions comes from Spiro's studies of Buddhism in Burma (1993). As presented by Spiro, one of the central doctrines of Theravada Buddhism is *Anatta*, "the doctrine that there is no Atman, or soul, alternatively ego, or transcendental self" (p. 119). In his studies of Burmese villagers, however, Spiro found that they strongly believe in the ego or soul. The reasons they do are twofold. First, the Burmese villagers do experience a subjective sense of self. The second reason stems from their inferences regarding incarnation. Believing that the quality of one's future existence is dependent on the merits of their present and past existences, it follows for them that there is a continuity of self (otherwise, they would not have to be concerned with the quality of their acts for future salvation).

Spiro's research illustrates how individuals' experiences and inferences can result in viewpoints different from official or public doctrines. It is also necessary to consider whether conceptions of persons are applied in different ways to different people. In much of the research the focus has been on persons "in general." When there is greater specification of persons in different positions in the social hierarchy, it turns out that individuals have multiple concepts of persons. In particular, independence is often attributed to males whereas dependence is attributed to females. Relevant studies were conducted among the Druze living in northern Israel (Wainryb and Turiel, 1994); the Druze constitute a traditional and patriarchal culture (see Turiel and Wainryb, 1994, for details). In these studies, individuals made judgments about how to make decisions when conflicts occur between family members regarding choices of activities (pertaining to education, work, leisure, friendships). The research showed that when a person in a dominant position (husband, father) objects to the choices of activities of a person in a subordinate position (wife, daughter) it is generally judged by both males and females that the person in the subordinate position should acquiesce (for example, a wife should not engage in an activity if her husband objects to it). These judgments were generally justified on grounds related to interdependence. By contrast, it was judged that a person in a dominant position need not and should not acquiesce in his chosen activities to objections from those in subordinate positions. These judgments were justified on the grounds of autonomy and independence. Specifically, autonomy and independence were attributed to males. In fact, the assumption that males have characteristics of independence resulted in the judgment that a son should not acquiesce to a father's objections to his chosen activities.

Another study with the Druze showed that members of the culture believe that independence is a psychological characteristic of males and interdependence is a characteristic of females. Most also believed that the culture shaped and called for these different psychologies—although for some, cultural shaping was seen as feeding into biological traits. In that study, people were posed questions about such activities as taking a job in a town different from their own or renting an apartment to live alone. Again, freedom to engage in the activities was associated with the sex of the actor. Males, who it was judged could engage in these activities, were described as free and self-reliant. As an example, a fourteen-year-old female thought it would be all right for a male to live alone: "Because in our culture a man is given complete freedom. No one would oppose a man being free. We like a man to be that way." Females were not described as self-reliant. This fourteen-year-old thought that a female should not live alone: "She can't establish herself on her own; she can't rely on herself. She needs someone to tell her what to do."

Along with concepts of persons as interdependent, therefore, there exist conceptions of persons as self-reliant, independent, and autonomous. As elaborated by Nucci (1996, 1997), the development of a sense of self, with boundaries and *spheres* of freedom and privacy, is not restricted to any particular culture. Furthermore, the development of a differentiated self is one of the bases for moral concepts of rights (Nucci, 1997). In many cultures, however, autonomy is not equally granted to people in different positions in the social hierarchy—between males and females or among members of different social classes. Independence and personal choices often are regarded as entitlements of those in positions of dominance. Among the Druze, for instance, there is a recognition and, to a fair extent, an acceptance of the greater independence and personal entitlements of males than females. Insofar as there is an acceptance of this type of division, there is an identification with the practices of the culture. However, coexisting with an identification with the culture is tension over the practices of that culture. The studies with the Druze also demonstrated that females had a different perspective on hierarchy from males. In particular, females made pragmatic judgments about the practices and judged them as unfair. Unlike males, females frequently thought that a person in a subordinate position should go along with the wishes of a person in a dominant position so as to avoid dire consequences (for example, a husband abandoning or divorcing his wife). Females also judged as unfair the lack of reciprocity in relationships.

These judgments on the part of Druze females indicate that people do evaluate their cultural practices from the moral point of view. The moral point of view, it has been found, includes in most cultures concepts of welfare and justice (see Miller, 1994; Shweder, Mahapatra, and Miller, 1987; Turiel, 1998). It also appears that concepts of rights are salient in Western and non-Western cultures (Helwig, 1995; Turiel and Wainryb, forthcoming). The same moral concepts that have been applied to "cultures" by those who espoused cultural relativism (such as tolerance, freedom, and equal worth) are held by members of most cultures. Therefore, members of most cultures are likely to apply concepts of tolerance and freedom to existing conditions of inequality, oppression, and the denial of rights within a culture.

Contested Meanings and Social Conflicts

Even though cultures are portrayed as cohesive and harmonious, it is also recognized that many Western societies, like the United States, are heterogeneous, include multiple viewpoints, and have their share of disagreements and conflicts. In all likelihood, few would disagree with Okin's contention (1989) that in the United States there are not shared understandings regarding gender issues. For those who maintain that cultures are cohesive, however, such disagreements are a consequence of the presence in the society of several cultural groups with different cultural practices. It is thought that these differences can lead to conflicts—conflicts that are sometimes referred to as culture wars. Moreover, it would be said that the assertion of rights and freedoms by women also reflects an extension of the culture's emphasis on individualism.

Consider the recollections of a woman writer (Gerber, 1997), as related in a newspaper column, of some of her experiences in the 1950s and 1960s. She recounts several examples of gender-based discrimination she (and other women) experienced, but about which she (and they) felt powerless to protest. With time, she realized that women could force changes in practices of domination and subordination: "It has taken too many years for us to figure out we don't have to tolerate, as a people, segregation, or discrimination. . . . Let us hope that in the future it won't take us as long as it has between the time we understand we deserve equal access to the entitlements of human life and the time it takes these freedoms to be afforded to all of us."

Explaining these types of cultural changes (though some maintain the changes have not been sufficient; see Okin, 1989) as a consequence of the presence of varying cultural groups in the society or as the extension of the society's individualism fails, in my view, to account for a fundamental source of conflict and change—namely, the tensions arising from relationships of dominance and subordination and an awareness of restrictions applied unequally in areas of personal agency. This is not to say that conflicts between different groups are irrelevant to change. Both Greenfield and Saxe (in Chapters Three and Two, respectively) demonstrate how the practices of traditional cultures (for example, in the technology of weaving and in the number system) have changed as a consequence of shifts in economic exchange and trade practices. Greenfield describes changes from farming to transportation business in Zinacantan, and Saxe points to the introduction, among the Oksapmin, of Western currency and trade stores (built by men who had returned to their community after working in other areas). As they clearly show, cultural changes and individuals' cognitive development can be influenced by the introduction of new practices from the outside.

Another source of change is from within. Cultures—including traditional ones—are not characterized by stability, recurrence, or intergenerational commonalities. Let me present a possible scenario that would give a somewhat different interpretation of events Greenfield (Chapter Three) describes for an agrarian community in 1970. Greenfield's interpretation is that the Zinacantec methods of teaching, with the goal of intergenerational replication of tradition, did not allow room for learner experimentation and discovery. Described is a teaching method whereby the teacher intervenes to provide direct guidance to the learner. An example is given of nine-year-old Katal, in 1970, being directly instructed by her mother. Changes in teaching practices from 1970 to 1990 are attributed to changes introduced in the economy. In the 1990s, Katal's own daughters were not taught directly to replicate tradition; rather, they learned independently and to innovate. I would suggest that one of the sources of the cultural changes might have been in the experiences of 1970, as well as in the experiences stemming from later economic changes. Though we cannot know now, it may be that learning on the part of children in 1970 was not as stable or as accepting as it may have appeared. Perhaps the nine-year-old Katal was not so ready to accept cultural practices as they existed and wished to innovate. If we wish to be fanciful about it, it could be imagined that a child like Katal, when her mother told her how to weave, might have said to herself, "Oh, no, here comes my mother again to tell me exactly what to do." With age, she (and her cohort) may have seized opportunities for innovation—innovations that, along with economic changes, produced transformations in cultural practices. This rendition of what may have transpired in the community of Zinacantan may or may not be accurate. I believe it is plausible, however. Children often do not express to adults their feelings of tension regarding cultural practices or social expectations.

Greater attention to generational differences might reveal conflicts that lead to substantive changes. As previously noted, greater attention needs to be given to the perspectives of those in nondominant positions in the social hierarchy. Those who have examined the perspectives of women in traditional cultures have shown that there is not always general acceptance of hierarchy and dominance (for example, Chen, 1995; Okin, 1989; Wikan, 1991). Within cultures there is conflict, struggle, and efforts at transforming social practices that place people at risk or that restrict their activities in ways judged unjust. The risks for people in subordinate positions can be associated with benefits for those in dominant positions; the restrictions in their activities can serve the desires and interests of people in positions of dominance. Discontents over such restrictions have been described for a range of issues, including ones that threaten people's survival and ones that prevent people from achieving many of their goals.

Dramatic examples of defiance of traditions and change motivated by survival needs in the realm of work have been described by Chen (1995), who worked with poor women in Bangladesh and India. In those circumstances, women "must break with tradition and act independently because they lack the security the tradition is supposed to offer. In communities where women are secluded, perhaps the most conspicuous, and yet necessary way for women to break with tradition is to leave their courtyards and homesteads in search of work" (Chen, 1995, p. 37). Leaving the courtyards or homesteads is not a simple task, as it violates cultural practices. According to Chen, sexual division of labor existed throughout the region, but until recently was more widely and uniformly enforced in Bangladesh than anywhere else. Women were excluded from fields, markets, roads, and towns (the public sphere of males) and confined to their huts and homesteads (the private sphere of females). *Purdah*, which designates appropriate behavior for women, involves "the seclusion of women within the boundaries of their homes and the veiling of women outside their homes" (Chen, 1995, p. 40). More broadly, "occupational purdah" designates appropriate and respectable work for women.

The changes in tradition brought about by acts of defiance by women were in response to needs for survival. In Bangladesh it was in reaction to the famine of 1974. Many women found themselves in the position of needing to provide the family with income because they were widows, their husbands were invalids, or their husbands could not earn enough. In those contexts, many women defied tradition and sought work provided by government programs. At first they had to work surreptitiously, eventually engaging in work openly, organizing, and publicly advocating for opportunities for women's work. The result was a substantial increase in the female labor force in Bangladesh and a transformation in attitudes toward women's work (Chen, 1995). In India the problem is especially acute for higher-caste women who find themselves in need of work (for example, widows) but for whom restrictions against work are strongly enforced. The felt conflict is between traditional family structure and financial needs. As put by Chen (1995, p. 55): "Indeed, the evidence suggests that increasing numbers of women receive little, if any, social security from traditional family structure and must act independently in order to provide for their families. This reality poses a moral dilemma. . . . The demand that women be allowed to abandon seclusion and seek gainful employment outside the home should not be seen as an outside challenge to local culture and tradition but as a local response to changes in local culture and tradition."

Beyond Survival

Economic forces are strong in people's lives, sometimes producing transformation in cultural practices. Economic influences can be from the outside but often also come from within. It may not be too surprising that changes from within experienced as threatening to one's needs for survival (as in Bangladesh) will produce efforts at defiance and transformation of traditions. However, internal conflicts persist because the counterreactions to defiance in the direction of preserving the traditions are also very strong. Moreover, this pattern of conflict, defiance, and counterresistance is not restricted to matters economic or those threatening survival. It occurs with regard to everyday activities regulated by cultural practices by which one group of people restricts and controls the activities of another group.

Conflicts and acts of defiance occur because relationships of power and dominance most often are not simply subsumed by duties based on asymmetrical reciprocity or an ideology of interdependence. As documented in the research with the Druze, these are differences in perspectives on cultural practices between those in dominant and subordinate positions. There is both a shared identification with the culture (in the form of an acknowledgment of the dominance of males and acceptance of their personal entitlements) and potential clashes in perceived vulnerabilities and injustices (in that women's acceptance of male dominance was based on fear of consequences and in that they judged practices as unfair).

There are several sources documenting that in traditional cultures there are contested views and conflicts. Contested views emerge from reports of people's hidden activities—hidden from those in positions of dominance—involving violations of socially expected behavior and even subversive activities (recall that Chen reported that women worked first in ways hidden from the community). Hidden activities on the part of women and efforts at transforming the ways women were restricted by cultural practices are the emphases of Mernissi's recollections (1994) of her life as a young girl during the 1940s in a harem in Morocco. As recollected by Mernissi, the women of the harem considered many of the rules and traditions unfair and felt them to be "suffocating." Practices such as polygamy and wearing of the veil were regarded as particularly onerous because they stigmatized women and served to deny rights. The title of Mernissi's book, *Dreams of Trespass,* connotes that the women desired, and even were obsessed with, going beyond the gates of the harem. The women also aspired to have their daughters live with greater freedoms and opportunities for education. The women did transgress in their daily lives, often engaging in prohibited activities in hidden ways. As an example, Mernissi recounts a vivid recollection from her childhood. Women were not allowed access to a radio in the men's salon; it was kept locked in a cabinet. Nevertheless, the women regularly listened to the radio while the men were away. One day, it was revealed that an "unlawful" key existed when, as children, Mernissi and her cousin were asked by her father what they had done that day. Upon hearing from the children that they had listened to the radio, the men embarked on two days of interrogation of the women to ascertain who had the key. The men were unsuccessful in their quest. Nevertheless, the women were angry with the children, accusing them of being traitors and instructing them that telling the truth was not always the right thing to do.

A similar message regarding the keeping of secrets and truth telling was expressed by a woman living in a different place and time. In 1997, an Iranian woman stated, "We live a double life in this country. My children know that when their school teachers ask whether we drink at home, they have to say no. If they are asked whether we dance or play cards, they have to say no. But the fact is that we do drink, dance and play cards, and the kids know it. So they are growing up as liars, knowing that their parents are also liars and knowing that to survive in this country we have to be. That's a terrible thing, and I want to change it" (Kinzer, 1997a). Although the social and political contexts of Iran differ from those of the harem in Morocco, in each case the example illustrates that there are networks of oppositional activities and conspiracies among those restricted by people in more powerful positions. Children receive mixed messages from adults (for example, about truth and lies), who seek cultural changes. The comments by the Iranian woman were made in the aftermath of the presidential elections of 1997. The cleric who had been elected president was considered more moderate than his opponents or previous presidents. It was felt by many that his election represented a shift to greater freedom, reflecting a desire by many that intrusions into people's private lives be removed. As put by one man: "The voters are saying that we are tired of people snooping into our private lives. What we do at home is our own business. With Khatami in power, the government is going to stop telling us what we can read, what we can watch and what we can do" (Kinzer, 1997b, p. A1). Even though the government and religious authorities attempt to tell people what to do, many engage in hidden activities in opposition to them. The hidden activities go beyond dancing, playing cards, and drinking at home. Those activities include dress, makeup, use of prohibited forms of entertainment (for example, television, compact discs), public contact between unmarried males and females, and even sexuality (for examples from other Islamic nations, see Goodwin, 1994).

The harems of Morocco in the 1940s and Iran of the 1990s constitute different historical and cultural contexts. Nevertheless, in each setting people live double lives. The commonalities between the two settings include the existence of conflicts and subversive activities. In each, there are efforts at changing practices that involve either restrictions, considered unfair, imposed by one group upon another, or intrusions upon activities that are considered legitimately within private and personal spheres. There is also research documenting the presence of these types of dynamics in still another traditional culture. Abu-Lughod (1993) has conducted ethnographic studies in Egypt of women living in Bedouin communities. The Bedouins, too, have a patriarchal social structure, with practices that restrict women's dress, leisure activities, education, and work. Bedouin women are part of the life of the culture, yet they resist and defy many social expectations. For example, women develop strategies to prevent marriages arranged for them and even provoke an unwanted husband to divorce. Women support each other in averting, when possible, husbands taking more than one wife—a practice disapproved of by many women. Polygamy is seen as part of the self-interested, self-indulgent, and exploitative behavior of males. Males are not simply considered superior beings who take care of others and who should be obeyed. They are seen by Bedouin women as individuals with human needs and foibles, who often use their positions of power and status for their own ends (Abu-Lughod, 1993). To show how individuals are aware of the self-serving uses of cultural arrangements, I quote from an interview with a fourteen-year-old Druze male (derived from a different study): "Look, it would be better for me if everything stayed this way. I can see from the viewpoint of a girl, she would like a change, like equality with boys. She would like to have the same rights. But of course everyone just wants what is best for themselves. And this situation, the way things are now, this is better for me, this is better for men. I can see, though, that for girls it would be much better if they had more freedom and more rights."

Conclusions

The sources of cultural change are broader and deeper than the presence of different cultural groups within society or the introduction of new events from the outside. Sources of change are ever present and linked to the makeup of social organization, to the nature of social relationships, and to the development of the thought of individuals. In other chapters in this volume there is discussion of how new events influence change (Edelstein, Saxe, and Greenfield) and of moral variations within cultures (Holloway). I have focused on the ways people's moral and personal judgments have impact on the nature of social relationships. Even traditional cultures are not characterized by stability, uniformity, or the absence of experimentation and novelty (Appadurai, 1988). Potential conflicts, variations, and innovative ideas exist because everyone does not participate in collective life in the same ways. Cultural practices affect people of different positions in different ways. As a consequence, the application of moral judgments to everyday situations may result in perceived needs for change on the part of those who are treated unequally, or those whose personal autonomy is seriously restricted, or those who are oppressed.

For these reasons, it is not all that informative simply to list ways in which cultures differ in their approval or disapproval of particular acts or practices. The usual litany of variations in social practices may, indeed, reflect cultural differences. For instance, in most Western cultures, practices like polygamy, arranged marriages, and the wearing of the veil are not accepted. We know that these are some of the publicly valued practices of some cultures. As we have seen, however, these are also practices over which there are conflicts, tensions, and struggles. The oppositional activities regarding those practices are often hidden or indirectly expressed. Sometimes the oppositional activities remain underground because of the actor's lack of power and fear of consequences. Sometimes they remain underground because of ambivalences. And even though people may make negative moral evaluations of particular practices, they also identify with the culture.

Moral evaluations of the practices are made from within. Frequently, underground activities emerge on the surface as indigenous movements for change (for documentation see Goodwin, 1994; Nussbaum and Glover, 1995; Walker and Parnar, 1993). Insofar as some of the ways of a culture (any culture, Western or non-Western) are judged from within, it must be said that cultures are open to moral critique. Just as cultural relativists called for an appreciation of the validity of the goals and values of a people and for the universal application of norms of tolerance, freedom, and equality, it can be said that the same considerations should be granted to groups of people in subordinate positions within cultures. The idea that moral judgments apply to relationships between people in dominant and subordinate positions is not limited to a particular moral philosophical perspective. Moral philosophical perspectives that have been extended to analyses of gender and social class inequalities include ones based on human capabilities (Nussbaum, 1995) and justice (Okin, 1989, 1995). In the context of Aristotelian conceptions of the good life, Nussbaum has articulated a set of capabilities for the good life that societies should aim to achieve for all citizens. Okin has extended theories of justice, like that of Rawls (1971), to gender relationships in the family in Western (Okin, 1989) and non-Western settings (Okin, 1995). Of most importance is that members of Western and non-Western cultures themselves are concerned with how social arrangements bear on personal goals and justice.

References

Abu-Lughod, L. "Writing Against Culture." In R. E. Fox (ed.), *Recapturing Anthropology: Working in the Present.* Santa Fe, N.M.: School of American Research Press, 1991.

Abu-Lughod, L. *Writing Women's Worlds: Bedouin Stories.* Berkeley: University of California Press, 1993.

Appadurai, A. "Putting Hierarchy in Its Place." *Cultural Anthropology,* 1988, *3,* 36–49.

Benedict, R. *Patterns of Culture.* Boston: Houghton Mifflin, 1934.
Chen, M. "A Matter of Survival: Women's Right to Employment India and Bangladesh." In M. C. Nussbaum and J. Glover (eds.), *Women, Culture, and Development: A Study of Human Capabilities.* New York: Oxford University Press, 1995.
Freud, S. *Civilization and Its Discontents.* New York: Norton, 1930.
Geertz, C. "From the Natives' Point of View: On the Nature of Anthropological Understanding." In R. A. Shweder and R. A. Levine (eds.), *Culture Theory: Essays on Mind, Self, and Emotion.* New York: Cambridge University Press, 1984.
Gerber, M. J. "A Long Road to Women's Freedoms." *San Francisco Chronicle,* June 30, 1997, p. A23.
Goodwin, J. *Price of Honor: Muslim Women Lift the Veil of Silence on the Islamic World.* New York: Plume/Penguin, 1994.
Hatch, E. *Culture and Morality: The Relativity of Values in Anthropology.* New York: Columbia University Press, 1983.
Helwig, C. C. "Adolescents' and Young Adults' Conceptions of Civil Liberties: Freedom of Speech and Religion." *Child Development,* 1995, 66, 152–166.
Herskovitz, M. J. *Man and His Works.* New York: Knopf, 1947.
Kinzer, S. "Beating the System with Bribes and the Big Lie." *New York Times,* May 27, 1997a, p. A4.
Kinzer, S. "Many Iranians Hope Mandate Brings Change." *New York Times,* May 26, 1997b, pp. A1, A4.
Kitayama, S., and Markus, H. R. *Emotion and Culture: Empirical Studies of Mutual Influence.* Washington, D.C.: American Psychological Association, 1994.
Markus, H. R., and Kitayama, S. "Culture and the Self: Implications for Cognition, Emotion, and Motivation." *Psychological Review,* 1991, 98, 224–253.
Mernissi, F. *Dreams of Trespass: Tales of a Harem Childhood.* Reading, Mass.: Addison-Wesley, 1994.
Miller, J. G. "Cultural Psychology: Bridging Disciplinary Boundaries in Understanding the Cultural Grounding of Self." In P. K. Bock (ed.), *Handbook of Psychological Anthropology.* Westport, Conn.: Greenwood Press, 1994.
Nucci, L. P. "Morality and the Personal Sphere of Action." In E. Reed, E. Turiel, and T. Brown (eds.), *Values and Knowledge.* Mahwah, N.J.: Erlbaum, 1996.
Nucci, L. P. "Culture, Context, and the Psychological Sources of Human Rights Concepts." Paper presented at the Conference on Morality in Context, Ringberg, Germany, July 29, 1997.
Nussbaum, M. C. "Human Capabilities, Female Human Beings." In M. C. Nussbaum and J. Glover (eds.), *Women, Culture, and Development: A Study of Human Capabilities.* New York: Oxford University Press, 1995.
Nussbaum, M. C., and Glover, J. (eds.). *Women, Culture, and Development: A Study of Human Capabilities.* New York: Oxford University Press, 1995.
Okin, S. M. *Justice, Gender, and the Family.* New York: Basic Books, 1989.
Okin, S. M. "Gender Inequality and Cultural Differences." In M. C. Nussbaum and J. Glover (eds.), *Women, Culture, and Development: A Study of Human Capabilities.* New York: Oxford University Press, 1995.
Piaget, J. *The Moral Judgment of the Child.* New York: Routledge, 1932.
Rawls, J. *A Theory of Justice.* Cambridge, Mass.: Harvard University Press, 1971.
Schmidt, P. H. "Some Criticisms of Cultural Relativism." *Journal of Philosophy,* 1955, 52, 780–791.
Shweder, R. A., and Haidt, J. "The Future of Moral Psychology: Truth, Intuition, and the Pluralist Way." *Psychological Science,* 1993, 4, 360–365.
Shweder, R. A., Mahapatra, M., and Miller, J. G. "Culture and Moral Development." In J. Kagan and S. Lamb (eds.), *The Emergence of Morality in Young Children.* Chicago: University of Chicago Press, 1987.

Shweder, R. A., Much, N. C., Mahapatra, M., and Park, L. "The 'Big Three' of Morality (Autonomy, Community, and Divinity) and the 'Big Three' Explanations of Suffering." In A. Brandt and P. Rozin (eds.), *Morality and Health.* New York: Routledge, 1997.

Skinner, B. F. *Beyond Freedom and Dignity.* New York: Knopf, 1971.

Spiro, M. "Is the Western Conception of the Self 'Peculiar' Within the Context of the World Cultures?" *Ethos,* 1993, *21,* 107–153.

Strauss, C. "Models and Motives." In R. G. D'Andrade and C. Strauss (eds.), *Human Motives and Cultural Models.* New York: Cambridge University Press, 1992.

Triandis, H. C. "Cross-Cultural Studies of Individualism and Collectivism." In J. J. Berman (ed.), *Nebraska Symposium on Motivation, 1989.* Vol. 37: *Cross-Cultural Perspectives.* Lincoln: University of Nebraska Press, 1990.

Triandis, H. C. "The Psychological Measurement of Cultural Syndromes." *American Psychologist,* 1996, *51,* 407–415.

Turiel, E. "The Development of Morality." In W. Damon (ed.), *Handbook of Child Psychology* (5th ed.). Vol. 3: *Social, Emotional, and Personality Development* (N. Eisenberg, ed.). New York: Wiley, 1998.

Turiel, E., and Wainryb, C. "Social Reasoning and the Varieties of Social Experience in Cultural Contexts." In H. W. Reese (ed.), *Advances in Child Development and Behavior.* Vol. 25. New York: Academic Press, 1994.

Turiel, E., and Wainryb, C. "Concepts of Freedoms and Rights in a Traditional Heirarchically Organized Society." *British Journal of Developmental Psychology,* forthcoming.

Wainryb, C., and Turiel, E. "Dominance, Subordination, and Concepts of Personal Entitlements in Cultural Contexts." *Child Development,* 1994, *65,* 1701–1722.

Walker, A., and Parnar, P. *Warrior Marks: Female Genital Mutilation and the Sexual Blinding of Women.* Orlando, Fla.: Harcourt Brace, 1993.

Wikan, U. "Toward an Experience-Near Anthropology." *American Anthropologist,* 1991, *6,* 285–305.

ELLIOT TURIEL is Chancellor's Professor in the Graduate School of Education at the University of California, Berkeley.

Index

Abu-Lughod, L., 2, 4, 80, 89, 90
Accommodation, and cognitive progress, 15
Adorno, T. W., 6, 8, 15, 16
Anthropology, cultural, 2, 79–80
Appadurai, A., 2, 4, 80, 89, 90
Aristotle, 90
Arithmetic, cognitive development in, 22–31
Artifacts, cultural change in, 41–42, 48–49
Assimilation, and cognitive progress, 11, 14
Azuma, H., 70, 74

Babylonia, mathematics in, 9
Bangladesh, cultural change in, 86–87
Benedict, R., 2, 4, 79, 90
Bennett, T., 32n
Benveniste, E., 8, 16
Berlyne, D. E., 14, 16
Body-part counting system, 21, 22–31
Body-part substitution strategy, 26, 28, 29
Boocock, S. S., 62, 74
Brazelton, T. B., 40, 58
Bruner, J. S., 15, 16, 37, 58
Burma, self and others in, 82

California at Los Angeles, University of, 37n
Cancian, F., 47, 58
Caputo, J. D., 6, 16
Challenge, in role-centered preschools, 69
Chandler, M., 6, 16
Change: cognitive context of, 5–17; and cognitive development, 19–35; cultural, 37–59, 77–92; directional or progressive, 58, 79; historical, 7
Chen, M., 78, 86–87, 91
Childs, C. P., 37n, 40, 41, 42n, 43, 44, 47, 48, 54, 58, 59
Cognition: moral, 8, 13; and sociocultural objects, 9
Cognitive development: in arithmetic, 22–31; aspects of, 19–35; concepts in, 19–20; conclusion on, 34; with fractions, 32–34; levels of analysis for, 20–34

Cognitive progress: aspects of, 5–17; attention to, 5–8; and division of labor and universal education, 12–14; evidence for, 15–16; and invariant numbers, 8–9; in logic and perspectivism, 9–12; and segmentation, 14–15
Cognitive representation, cultural change in, 41–47, 55
Cole, M., 19, 35
Collectivities, 1–2
Competence, segmentation of, 7–8, 14–15
Complexity, impact of, 5–6, 15
Conflict: and cultural change, 77–92; in role-centered preschools, 71–73
Conroy, M., 70, 74
Constructivism, 1, 20
Contextualism, 6
Control, in role-centered preschools, 70–71
Cultural change: aspects of, 37–59, 77–92; background on, 77–78; comparisons for, 78–81; conclusions on, 57–58, 89–90; contested meanings and conflicts in, 84–88; cross-cultural studies of, 37–38; cross-generational study of, 38–57, 85–86; dissent and seams in, 81–84; and first generation, 40–47; and next generation, 47–57; and survival, 87–89; theory of, 39
Cultural models: concept of, 63–64; of preschools, 64–66
Cultural practices: and cognitive development, 19–35; of economic exchange, 20–22
Cultural relativism, 79–80, 90
Culture and development: and change, 5–59; coherence of, 79–80; and diversity, 61–92; overview of, 1–4
Currency, and cognitive development, 22, 24–25
Curtius, E. R., 12, 16

Damerow, P., 7, 8–9, 16
Davidson, D. H., 62, 72, 75
Décalage, in Middle Ages, 12
Derrida, J., 6, 16
Development. *See* Cognitive development; Culture and development; Social development

Development, Evolution, and Culture symposium, 37n
Devereaux, L., 37n, 47
Dewey, J., 14
Discovery learning, and cultural change, 51, 53
Diversity: aspects of, 61–92; and cultural change, 77–92; and integration, 2; intracultural, 63–64; in preschools, 61–75
Doi, T., 65, 74
Double-enumeration strategy, 26–27, 29
Durkheim, E., 5–6, 7, 13, 15, 16

Eaves, L. J., 57, 59
Economic exchange: and cultural practices, 20–22; and microgenesis, 24–25
Edelstein, W., 3, 5, 6, 7, 12, 13, 14, 15, 16, 17, 38, 78, 89
Education: ascendancy of universal, 12–14; and cognitive progress, 6, 7, 10–15; and cultural change, 40–41, 47, 56; moral, 13, 77–78, 90; in preschools, 61–75
Eggers-Pérola, C., 64, 74
Egypt, cultural change in, 89
El Colegio de la Frontera Sur, 37n
Elias, N., 12, 16
Epigenesis, 20

Feiler, B. S., 74
Fogarty International Center, 37n
Forms, cultural, and cognitive functions, 20, 22–31
Foucault, M., 8, 16
Fractions, cognitive development with, 32–34
Freud, S., 77, 91
Fuller, B., 64, 74
Functions, cognitive, and cultural forms, 20, 22–31

Garcia, R., 8, 16
Gearhart, M., 32, 35
Geertz, C., 82, 91
Gelman, R., 51
Gerber, M. J., 84–85, 91
Gjerde, P. F., 63, 74
Global enumeration procedure, 25, 29
Glover, J., 90, 91
Goodwin, J., 88, 90, 91
Greenfield, L., 47–48, 50n, 52n, 54n, 56n
Greenfield, P. M., 3, 19, 37, 38, 40, 41, 43, 44, 48, 51, 54, 55, 56, 58–59, 79, 85, 89

Greenfield, S., 40n, 44n, 49n, 51n
Growing Mind, 37n
Guilford, V., 30

Habermas, J., 7, 16
Hagen-Sepik patrol, 20–21
Haidt, J., 80, 91
Halved-body procedure, 28–29
Harkness, S., 58, 59
Harvard Center for Cognitive Studies, 37n
Harvard Medical School, Milton Fund of, 37n
Hatch, E., 2, 4, 79, 91
Heath, A. C., 57, 59
Helwig, C. C., 84, 91
Hendry, J., 62, 74
Herskovitz, M. J., 79, 91
Hess, R. D., 70, 74
History, and cognitive progress, 5–17
Holland, D., 63–64, 75
Holloway, S. D., 3, 61, 64, 74–75, 89
Horkheimer, M., 6, 8, 15, 16
Hybrid enumeration system, 31

Iceland, traditional patterns in, 12
India, cultural change in, 86–87
Interactionism, 1
Iran, cultural change in, 88, 89
Ishigaki, E. H., 62, 75
Israel, Druze in, 83–84, 87, 89

Japan, preschools in, 61–75
Jean Piaget Society, 37n

Kant, I., 6
Kaplan, B., 23, 35
Kashiwagi, K., 70, 74
Kasya, X., 43
Khatami, 88
Kinzer, S., 88, 91
Kitayama, S., 61, 75, 80, 91
Knowledge, structure of, 13
Kohei, 73
Kojima, H., 64, 75
Kondo, D. K., 61, 64, 73, 75
Kruger, A. C., 37, 59
Kuhn, T. S., 7, 16

Labor, division of, 12–14
Lancy, D. F., 21, 35
Lave, J., 40, 48, 51, 59
Learning, cultural change in, 41, 43, 49–55
Lewis, C. C., 62, 75

Litvinovic, G., 63, 75
Logic, in Middle Ages, 9–12
Luria, A. R., 19, 35, 38, 59

Magical thinking, and cognitive regression, 10
Mahapatra, M., 81, 84, 91–92
Markus, H. R., 61, 75, 80, 91
Maynard, A. E., 37n, 54, 56, 59
Mead, M., 2, 4
Mediation, and cognitive development, 20
Mernissi, F., 87–88, 91
Mesopotamia, invariant numbers in, 8–9
Mexico, cultural change in, 40–57, 85
Microgenesis: and body-part counting, 23–26; concept of, 20; and fractions, 32–33
Middle Ages, logic and perspectivism in, 9–12
Milgram, S., 7, 16
Miller, J. G., 81, 84, 91
Miller, M., 7, 16
Minami, M., 64, 75
Ministry of Education (Japan), 62, 65, 66, 69, 71
Morocco, cultural change in, 87–88, 89
Motivation, cognitive, 14–15
Mouer, R., 74, 75
Moylan, T., 30
Much, N. C., 81, 91–92

National Geographic Society, 37n, 48
National Institutes of Health, 37n
Neale, M. C., 57, 59
Nissen, H. J., 9, 17
Noam, G., 7, 16
Nucci, L. P., 83, 91
Numbers, invariant, 8–9
Numeration: strategies for, 25–31; traditional practices for, 20–22; vehicles and objects for, 23–24
Nussbaum, M. C., 90, 91

Okin, S. M., 78, 80, 82, 84, 85, 86, 90, 91
Oksapmin, counting by, 20–31
Olver, R. R., 38, 59
Ontogenesis: and body-part counting, 26–30; concept of, 20; and fractions, 33–34
Organization for Economic Cooperation and Development, 5, 17

Papua New Guinea, cultural practices in, 20–31, 38

Park, L., 81, 91–92
Parnar, P., 90, 92
Pavlu, A., 49
Pavlu, K., 40, 41, 43, 51, 53, 54, 85
Pavlu, L., 54
Pavlu, M., 49
Pavlu, S., 37n
Peak, L., 62, 65, 70, 72, 75
Pedagogy, in role-centered preschools, 68–69
Pelto, G. H., 63, 75
Pelto, P. J., 63, 75
Perspectivism, in Middle Ages, 9–12
Pérusse, D., 57, 59
Piaget, J., 1–2, 4, 7, 10, 14, 17, 20, 35, 51, 57, 59, 77, 91
Practices: concept of, 19–20; cultural, 19–35; social, 77–78, 90
Preschools: aspects of Japanese, 61–75; background on, 61–63; child-centered, 65, 68, 69, 70; conclusions on, 74; cultural models of, 64–66; goal of, 62; role-centered, 63, 65–73; society-centered, 65, 68, 70
Progressivism, cognitive, 5–17
Prussia, compulsory schooling in, 14

Quinn, C. J., Jr., 65, 75
Quinn, N., 63–64, 75

Radcliffe College, Bunting Institute at, 37n
Radding, C. M., 10–12, 17
Rambaud, M. F., 64, 74
Ratner, H. H., 37, 59
Rawls, J., 90, 91
Regression, cognitive, 6, 10
Reich, L. C., 38, 59
Relativism, cultural, 79–80, 90
Representation, cognitive, 41–47, 55
Rogoff, B., 37, 59
Rohlen, T. P., 74, 75
Role-centered preschools: challenge in, 69; characteristics of, 63, 65–66; conflict in, 71–73; control in, 70–71; pedagogy in, 68–69; portrait of, 66–73; self and other models in, 66–68

Santis, L., 53–54
Santis, X., 53–54
Saussure, F. de, 7, 17
Saxe, G. B., 3, 19, 20, 28, 32, 35, 37, 38, 39, 59, 79, 85, 89
Scaffolded learning, and cultural change, 41, 51, 57

Schmidt, P. H., 79, 91
Scribner, S., 19, 35, 39, 59
Segmentation, of competence, 7–8, 14–15
Self and others: and cultural change, 82–84; in preschools, 66–68
Seltzer, M., 32, 35
Senegal, cognitive development in, 38
Shweder, R. A., 6, 17, 80, 81, 84, 91–92
Skinner, B. F., 77, 92
Smith, H. W., 74, 75
Smith, R. J., 70, 75
Snow, Ms., 32–34
Social development, and cultural change, 77–92
Socialization: and cultural change, 39; in preschools, 61–75
Sociocognitive complexity, 5–6
Sociogenesis: and body-part counting, 30–31; concept of, 20; and fractions, 34
Solidarity, organic, 13, 15
Spencer Foundation, 37n
Spiro, M., 2, 4, 80, 82, 92
Staub, E., 7, 17
Stevenson, H. W., 61, 75
Stigler, J., 61, 75
Stipek, D. J., 32, 35
Strauss, C., 2, 4, 80, 92
Sugimoto, Y., 74, 75
Super, C. M., 58, 59
Symbolic tools, cultural change in, 47, 55–57

Tobin, J. J., 62, 72, 75

Tomasello, M., 37, 59
Tools, symbolic, cultural change in, 47, 55–57
Triandis, H. C., 77, 80, 92
Troubetckoy, N. S., 7, 17
Turiel, E., 3, 4, 37n, 77, 83, 84, 92

Union of Soviet Socialist Republics, collectivization in, 38

Valsinger, J., 63, 75
Vasquez family, 41
Vogt, E. Z., 40, 59
Vygotsky, L., 20, 35, 38, 51, 57, 59, 63

Wainryb, C., 83, 84, 92
Wakaba Preschool, 66–73
Walker, A., 90, 92
Waseda, Mr., 66–68, 71
Watanabe, Ms., 73
Weaving, cultural change in, 40–57, 85
Werner, H., 23, 35
Wertsch, J., 19, 35
White, R. W., 14, 17
Wikan, U., 2, 4, 80, 82, 86, 92
Wiswell, E. L., 70, 75
Wu, D.Y.H., 62, 72, 75

Yamagi, Mr., 70–71
Yut, E., 37n

Zinacantan, cultural change in, 40–57, 85

Errata

On societies other than India, the data reported in D. Sharma and R. A. LeVine, "Child Care in India," in D. Sharma and K. W. Fischer (eds.), *Socioemotional Development Across Cultures,* New Directions for Child Development, no. 81, San Francisco: Jossey-Bass, specifically Tables 3.5, 3.7, 3.8, 3.9, and 3.10 and the methods reported on pages 57–58 were drawn from A. Richman and others, "Maternal Behaviors in Five Cultures," in R. A. LeVine, P. M. Miller, M. M. West (eds.), *Parental Behavior in Diverse Societies,* New Directions for Child Development, no. 40, San Francisco: Jossey-Bass.

Please note that Ann C. Crouter's name was misspelled on the cover of *Temporal Rhythms in Adolescence: Clocks, Calendars, and the Coordination of Daily Life,* New Directions for Child Development, no. 82. Ann is spelled without an "e."

Back Issue/Subscription Order Form

Copy or detach and send to:
Jossey-Bass Inc., Publishers, 350 Sansome Street, San Francisco CA 94104-1342
Call or fax toll free!
Phone 888-378-2537 6AM–5PM PST; Fax 800-605-2665

Back issues: Please send me the following issues at $25 each.
(Important: please include series initials and issue number, such as CD82.)

1. CD _____

_____

_____

$ _____ Total for single issues

$ _____ Shipping charges (for single issues *only;* subscriptions are exempt from shipping charges): Up to $30, add $5^{50} • $30^{01}–$50, add $6^{50}
$50^{01}–$75, add $7^{50} • $75^{01}–$100, add $9 • $100^{01}–$150, add $10
Over $150, call for shipping charge.

Subscriptions   Please ❑ start   ❑ renew my subscription to *New Directions for Child and Adolescent Development* for the year 19___ at the following rate:

❑ Individual $67   ❑ Institutional $115
NOTE: Subscriptions are quarterly, and are for the calendar year only. Subscriptions begin with the spring issue of the year indicated above. For shipping outside the U.S., please add $25.

$ _____ Total single issues and subscriptions (CA, IN, NJ, NY and DC residents, add sales tax for single issues. NY and DC residents must include shipping charges when calculating sales tax. NY and Canadian residents only, add sales tax for subscriptions.)

❑ Payment enclosed (U.S. check or money order only)
❑ VISA, MC, AmEx, Discover Card #_____ Exp. date_____

Signature _____ Day phone _____
❑ Bill me (U.S. institutional orders only. Purchase order required.)
Purchase order #_____

Name _____
Address _____

_____

_____

Phone_____ E-mail _____

For more information about Jossey-Bass Publishers, visit our Web site at:
www.josseybass.com   **PRIORITY CODE = ND1**

OTHER TITLES AVAILABLE IN THE
NEW DIRECTIONS FOR CHILD AND ADOLESCENT DEVELOPMENT SERIES
William Damon, Editor-in-Chief

CD82	Temporal Rhythms in Adolescence: Clocks, Calendars, and the Coordination c Daily Life, *Ann C. Crouter, Reed W. Larson*
CD81	Socioemotional Development Across Cultures, *Dinesh Sharma, Kurt W. Fischer*
CD80	Sociometry Then and Now: Building on Six Decades of Measuring Children's Experiences with the Peer Group, *William M. Bukowski, Antonius H. Cillessen*
CD79	The Nature and Functions of Gesture in Children's Communication, *Jana M. Iverson, Susan Goldin-Meadow*
CD78	Romantic Relationships in Adolescence: Developmental Perspectives, *Shmuel Shulman, W. Andrew Collins*
CD77	The Communication of Emotion: Current Research from Diverse Perspectives, *Karen Caplovitz Barrett*
CD76	Culture as a Context for Moral Development, *Herbert D. Saltzstein*
CD75	The Emergence of Core Domains of Thought: Children's Reasoning About Physical, Psychological, and Biological Phenomena, *Henry M. Wellman, Kayoko Inagaki*
CD74	Understanding How Family-Level Dynamics Affect Children's Development: Studies of Two-Parent Families, *James P. McHale, Philip A. Cowan*
CD73	Children's Autonomy, Social Competence, and Interactions with Adults and Other Children: Exploring Connections and Consequences, *Melanie Killen*
CD72	Creativity from Childhood Through Adulthood: The Developmental Issues, *Mark A. Runco*
CD71	Leaving Home: Understanding the Transition to Adulthood, *Julia A. Graber, Judith Semon Dubas*
CD69	Exploring Young Children's Concepts of Self and Other Through Conversation, *Linda L. Sperry, Patricia A. Smiley*
CD68	African American Family Life: Its Structural and Ecological Aspects, *Melvin N. Wilson*
CD67	Cultural Practices as Contexts for Development, *Jacqueline J. Goodnow, Peggy J. Miller, Frank Kessel*
CD65	Childhood Gender Segregation: Causes and Consequences, *Campbell Leaper*
CD64	Children, Youth, and Suicide: Developmental Perspectives, *Gil G. Noam, Sophie Borst*
CD62	Father—Adolescent Relationships, *Shmuel Shulman, W. Andrew Collins*
CD61	The Development of Literacy Through Social Interaction, *Colette Daiute*
CD60	Close Friendships in Adolescence, *Brett Laursen*
CD59	The Role of Play in the Development of Thought, *Marc H. Bornstein, Anne Watson O'Reilly*
CD58	Interpretive Approaches to Children's Socialization, *William A. Corsaro, Peggy J. Miller*
CD57	Beyond the Parent: The Role of Other Adults in Children's Lives, *Robert C. Pianta*
CD55	Emotion and Its Regulation in Early Development, *Nancy Eisenberg, Richard A. Fabes*
CD53	Academic Instruction in Early Childhood: Challenge or Pressure? *Leslie Rescorla, Marion C. Hyson, Kathy Hirsh-Pasek*
CD52	Religious Development in Childhood and Adolescence, *Fritz K. Oser, W. George Scarlett*
CD46	Economic Stress: Effects on Family Life and Child Development, *Vonnie C. McLoyd, Constance Flanagan*
CD42	Black Children and Poverty: A Developmental Perspective, *Diana T. Slaughter*
CD40	Parental Behavior in Diverse Societies, *Robert A. LeVine, Patrice M. Miller, Mary Maxwell West*

UNITED STATES POSTAL SERVICE™

Statement of Ownership, Management, and Circulation
(Required by 39 USC 3685)

1. Publication Title: NEW DIRECTIONS FOR STUDENT SERVICES	2. Publication Number: 0164-7970	3. Filing Date: 10/14/98
4. Issue Frequency: QUARTERLY	5. Number of Issues Published Annually: 4	6. Annual Subscription Price: $56 - indiv. / $99 - instit.

7. Complete Mailing Address of Known Office of Publication (Not printer) (Street, city, county, state, and ZIP+4)
350 SANSOME STREET
SAN FRANCISCO, CA 94104
(SAN FRANCISCO COUNTY)

Contact Person: ROGER HUNT
Telephone: 415 782 3232

8. Complete Mailing Address of Headquarters or General Business Office of Publisher (Not printer)
SAME AS ABOVE

9. Full Names and Complete Mailing Addresses of Publisher, Editor, and Managing Editor (Do not leave blank)

Publisher (Name and complete mailing address)
JOSSEY-BASS INC., PUBLISHERS
(ABOVE ADDRESS)

Editor (Name and complete mailing address)
JOHN SCHUH, PROFESSOR
PROFESSIONAL STUDIES IN EDUCATION
IOWA STATE UNIV/LAGOMARCINO HALL N247E
AMES, IA 50011

Managing Editor (Name and complete mailing address)
NONE

10. Owner (Do not leave blank. If the publication is owned by a corporation, give the name and address of the corporation immediately followed by the names and addresses of all stockholders owning or holding 1 percent or more of the total amount of stock. If not owned by a corporation, give the names and addresses of the individual owners. If owned by a partnership or other unincorporated firm, give its name and address as well as those of each individual owner. If the publication is published by a nonprofit organization, give its name and address.)

Full Name	Complete Mailing Address
SIMON & SCHUSTER	P.O. BOX 1172
	ENGLEWOOD CLIFFS, NJ 07632-1172

11. Known Bondholders, Mortgagees, and Other Security Holders Owning or Holding 1 Percent or More of Total Amount of Bonds, Mortgages, or Other Securities. If none, check box. ☐ None

Full Name	Complete Mailing Address
SAME AS ABOVE	SAME AS ABOVE

12. Tax Status (For completion by nonprofit organizations authorized to mail at special rates) (Check one)
The purpose, function, and nonprofit status of this organization and the exempt status for federal income tax purposes:
☐ Has Not Changed During Preceding 12 Months
☐ Has Changed During Preceding 12 Months (Publisher must submit explanation of change with this statement)

PS Form 3526, September 1995 (See Instructions on Reverse)

---

13. Publication Title: NEW DIRECTIONS FOR STUDENT SERVICES
14. Issue Date for Circulation Data Below: FALL 1998

15. Extent and Nature of Circulation		Average No. Copies Each Issue During Preceding 12 Months	Actual No. Copies of Single Issue Published Nearest to Filing Date
a. Total Number of Copies (Net press run)		1892	1902
b. Paid and/or Requested Circulation	(1) Sales Through Dealers and Carriers, Street Vendors, and Counter Sales (Not mailed)	207	47
	(2) Paid or Requested Mail Subscriptions (Include advertiser's proof copies and exchange copies)	786	846
c. Total Paid and/or Requested Circulation (Sum of 15b(1) and 15b(2))		993	893
d. Free Distribution by Mail (Samples, complimentary, and other free)		0	0
e. Free Distribution Outside the Mail (Carriers or other means)		140	76
f. Total Free Distribution (Sum of 15d and 15e)		140	76
g. Total Distribution (Sum of 15c and 15f)		1133	969
h. Copies not Distributed	(1) Office Use, Leftovers, Spoiled	759	933
	(2) Returns from News Agents	0	0
i. Total (Sum of 15g, 15h(1), and 15h(2))		1892	1902
Percent Paid and/or Requested Circulation (15c / 15g x 100)		88%	92%

16. Publication of Statement of Ownership
☒ Publication required. Will be printed in the WINTER 1998 issue of this publication.
☐ Publication not required.

17. Signature and Title of Editor, Publisher, Business Manager, or Owner
SUSAN E. LEWIS
DIRECTOR OF PERIODICALS
Date: 10/14/98

I certify that all information furnished on this form is true and complete. I understand that anyone who furnishes false or misleading information on this form or who omits material or information requested on the form may be subject to criminal sanctions (including fines and imprisonment) and/or civil sanctions (including multiple damages and civil penalties).

Instructions to Publishers

1. Complete and file one copy of this form with your postmaster annually on or before October 1. Keep a copy of the completed form for your records.
2. In cases where the stockholder or security holder is a trustee, include in Items 10 and 11 the name of the person or corporation for whom the trustee is acting. Also include the names and addresses of individuals who are stockholders who own or hold 1 percent or more of the total amount of bonds, mortgages, or other securities of the publishing corporation. In Item 11, if none, check the box. Use blank sheets if more space is required.
3. Be sure to furnish all circulation information called for in Item 15. Free circulation must be shown in Items 15d, e, and f.
4. If the publication had second-class authorization as a general or requester publication, this Statement of Ownership, Management, and Circulation must be published; it must be printed in any issue in October or, if the publication is not published during October, the first issue printed after October.
5. In Item 16, indicate the date of the issue in which this Statement of Ownership will be published.
6. Item 17 must be signed.

Failure to file or publish a statement of ownership may lead to suspension of second-class authorization.